POVERTY IN AMERICA

LOWELL GALLAWAY

Ohio University
Athens, Ohio

TABLE OF CONTENTS

PREFACE

Every book has its own unique history. This volume really had its inception almost a decade ago at the time at which the "poverty question" arose as an important issue in American society. At that time, I was employed at the Social Security Administration's Baltimore, Maryland offices and my first real exposure to the poverty problem was through a review of three significant books on the subject that was brought to my attention by another staff member. The analysis contained in that review was sufficiently erroneous to inspire my first serious investigations into the nature and sources of poverty in America. Since then, I have been periodically drawn back to the subject until finally we have this volume.

Along the path to this point a number of people have made significant contributions to my thinking, but none more than my late colleague, Gene L. Chapin. He and I had discussed the possibility of writing a book dealing with the poverty question for some time, but the press of other projects and the like always seemed to prevent our accomplishing this task. In fact, were it not for his untimely death at age 29 last March (1972), this book probably would still be just in the discussion stage. However, because of his passing, I unexpectedly found myself teaching our course in the Economics of Poverty for a second successive year. Very frankly, I was so unhappy with the material available for use in that course that I began to assemble these chapters. And, as I did, a general theme emerged, one that dominates this book, namely, the significance of differences in the genetic endowments that people possess as an explanation for variations in individual economic status. The importance of this factor has led me, as far as I know, to use the expression "genetic human capital" for the first time.

The emphasis on genetic factors as an explanation for differential economic status has led me down some paths that have been personally unpleasant and have caused me to give pause as to whether I really wished to pursue this inquiry to its logical conclusion. That raises an extremely difficult question. Is it really appropriate for a scholar to take it upon himself to decide, on moral grounds, whether the results of his scholarly inquiries should be made public? My own view is that he should not. Screening one's own research results to insure their moral acceptability to one's self is simply not consistent with maintaining any semblance of objectivity. And, one must be a purist in this respect. It is not possible to turn objectivity on and off at will. Once a scholar consciously compromises himself in this fashion, he is permanently tarnished. There is no such thing as being "just slightly non-objective" or "almost always objective."

To avoid misinterpretation, let me clarify what I mean by objectivity. It does not imply that one's conclusions are always valid. Objectivity does not mean infallibility. What it does involve, though, is an honest effort to arrive at valid answers to scholarly questions *independent of one's own personal preferences*. But, who is to determine whether someone has maintained objectivity in his analysis of a particular problem? In all candor, this is a distinctly personal problem. Certainly, others (both scholars and non-scholars) will form their judgment on this point. Ultimately, however, the critical appraisal of objectivity must be made by the scholar himself in an introspective fashion. Only he really knows whether he has been as objective as he should be and, in the final analysis, he is accountable primarily to himself. In a very real sense, the cliche "to thine own self be true" is appropriate here. All I can say at this point is that I think I have been honest and objective in the writing of this book.

So much for the preliminaries: Let us get on with the substantive analysis of the phenomenon of poverty in America.

Athens, Ohio
January 1973

POVERTY IN PERSPECTIVE

Poverty in America was "rediscovered" in the early 1960's. Suddenly, in the midst of the affluence of the post-World War II period, there was an "awakening" to the possibility that unacceptably low levels of income existed among significant numbers of people. This theme was rather eloquently articulated by a variety of social scientists and social critics; and, might I add, in an extremely effective fashion. Perhaps the best measure of how well they made their point is the simple observation that the primary thrust of Lyndon Johnson's first major policy speech upon assuming the presidency was the inauguration of the "War on Poverty."

The emergence of the poverty issue at this point in time raises some interesting questions, the most obvious one being, "Why then?" Was there anything unique about the United States as it entered the decade of the '60's that would account for a sudden "rediscovery" of poverty? According to John Kenneth Galbraith, one of the more prominent commentators on the poverty issue, the answer to that question is clearly affirmative. In his view, poverty had become a special or relatively isolated phenomenon in the post-World War II world. By contrast, he implies that earlier in the history of the United States poverty was a generalized, or majority, phenomenon. And Galbraith is not alone in this view. It is relatively easy to find statements in the poverty literature that suggest contemporary poverty may be distinguished from earlier poverty by its lack of general pervasiveness.

The contention that poverty has become a minority rather than a majority phenomenon has intriguing implications. At first glance, it might seem that this is a positive step, for it clearly argues that the level of poverty in the United States has been reduced. However, this is not the Galbraithian interpretation. Instead, it is argued that being poor when poverty is a minority thing is a more traumatic and damaging blow to the spirit than being poor in a world in which being poor is the normal condition. Thus, the "intensity of suffering" of the contemporary poor may well exceed that of the poor when poverty was more widely spread. This is an interesting proposition, although it is virtually impossible to either confirm or deny it on the basis of empirical evidence. In its own way, it is simply the application of the "misery loves company" cliche to the contemporary poverty question.

From an analytical standpoint, the "intensity of suffering" aspect of current poverty has little to offer us. However, the argument that poverty is no longer the majority condition has other implications that are quite far reaching and are also useful analytically. For example, while it may not be obvious at this point, the very validity of the "new" view of poverty turns crucially on (1) how poverty is defined and (2) historical changes in the pattern of income distribution in the United States. We will now proceed to explore these in more detail.

I. THE ABSOLUTE APPROACH TO DEFINING POVERTY

To begin, it is rather easy to accept the basic proposition that poverty has become a minority phenomenon if a definition of poverty is adopted that views it as existing when income falls below some absolute level deemed to be sufficient to permit a minimal subsistence standard of living.[3] Clearly, if such a definition is employed, sustained general economic growth will operate to increase income levels through time and pull people across whatever income boundary is felt to be the appropriate one for determining whether one is in poverty, unless, of course, none of the impact of economic growth is felt by those with incomes below the assumed poverty level.

We will ignore this possibility for the moment on the grounds that if it were true historically, poverty would have remained a majority phenomenon.

Following the line of reasoning already suggested, we can see clearly from the data of Table 1 how the process of economic growth could operate to alter the relative importance of poverty in the society. For purposes of discussion, assume that $3,000 of family income (in 1963 prices) is an acceptable dividing line between poverty and non-poverty. We make no particular case for the legitimacy of this definition. Any level of income markedly less than the present median family income would suffice. However, this particular choice is reasonably consistent with the "official" definitions employed by the Federal Government.[4] Using this absolute definition of a poverty level of income, the proportion of families in poverty was approximately one third in the immediate post-World War II period as compared to about one-ninth currently. Extrapolating backwards to 1935-36 we find that the median level of family income (in 1963 prices) was slightly over $2,500 or *less than the $3,000 poverty definition*.[5] Thus, using the $3,000 dividing line, poverty was the order of the day in the United States prior to World War II.

The overall impression one obtains from this view of the poverty issue is that a substantial and meaningful change in the nature of poverty in American society has occurred, largely as the result of sustained economic growth. Projecting ahead, this would seem to imply that future economic growth would tend to have a similar effect, i.e., further substantial reductions in the level of poverty in the society. Ah, but there's the rub! The bulk of the discussion that emerged in the early

Table 1

PERCENT OF FAMILIES WITH LESS THAN $3,000 ANNUAL INCOME [1963 PRICES], MEDIAN FAMILY INCOME [1957-59 PRICES], AND UNEMPLOYMENT RATE, UNITED STATES, 1947-1970

Year	Percent of Families with less than $3,000 Annual Income	Median Family Income	Unemployment Rate
1947	31.7%	$ 3,896	3.9%
1950	31.2	3,961	5.3
1953	25.8	4,542	2.9
1954	27.4	4,458	5.6
1955	24.4	4,738	4.4
1956	22.2	5,051	4.2
1957	22.2	5,072	4.3
1958	22.5	5,052	6.8
1959	21.4	5,337	5.5
1960	20.9	5,451	5.6
1961	20.9	5,506	6.7
1962	19.7	5,651	5.6
1963	18.5	5,856	5.7
1964	17.9	6,077	5.2
1965	16.8	6,330	4.5
1966	15.2	6,631	3.8
1967	14.2	6,829	3.8
1968	12.8	7,122	3.6
1969	12.5	7,387	3.5
1970	13.1	7,295	4.9

Sources: Department of Commerce, U.S. Bureau of the Census, *Current Population Reports*, P-60 Series. Washington, D.C.: U.S.G.P.O., various years, and Department of Labor, *Manpower Report of the President* Washington, D.C.: U.S.G.P.O., March 1972.

1960's argued very strongly that this would not be the case.[6] Rather, it was quite vigorously maintained that we were approaching a point beyond which much less could be expected in the way of reductions in the poverty rate if we relied solely on economic growth as a device for eliminating poverty. Perhaps as clear a statement as any of this position is the following quote from the Economic Report of the President:[7]

> [The] facts suggest that in the future economic growth alone will provide relatively fewer escapes from poverty. Policy will have to be more sharply focused on the handicaps that deny the poor fair access to the expanding incomes of a growing economy.

This is a position that has frequently been called the "backwash hypothesis." Essentially, it argues that there is a significant minority of people in the United States who are relatively unaffected by what happens in general in the economy. Independent of whether there are high levels of aggregate demand for goods and services and low levels of unemployment, poverty persists for these members of the society. They simply are left behind by the remainder of the population and are not in the "mainstream" of contemporary activity. Thus, the "backwash" notion. From a policy standpoint, this suggests the need for special selective programs aimed directly at improving the economic lot of the poor.

At this point, one may ask, "Why the difference in the relationship between the poverty rate and economic growth now as compared to the past?" When first suggested, i.e., in the early 1960's, the "backwash" hypothesis existed in an intellectual milieu that was quite congenial to the notion that significant structural changes were occurring in the American economy. Economists, both academic and non-academic, were deeply involved in the so-called "structural unemployment" controversy. That argument turned on whether there was a long term tendency for aggregate unemployment rates to increase due to structural changes in the economy. At the heart of this contention was the idea that such developments as increasing educational requirements for employment and/or automation were operating to "disenfranchise" people from the labor market. Put very simply, this is merely the backwash idea applied to the more limited sphere of employment. Philosophically, the backwash and structural unemployment hypotheses have the same basic roots, namely, a belief that fundamental and sweeping changes in the nature of the American economy were occurring at mid-century. Our purpose at this point is not to pass judgment on the legitimacy of this proposition (that will be done later), but merely to articulate the basic arguments that have been made in order to facilitate later analysis.

II. THE RELATIVE APPROACH TO DEFINING POVERTY

The utility of the view of poverty presented thus far lies in its offering a coherent set of propositions and hypotheses with respect to (1) why contemporary poverty differs from historical poverty and (2) why a different basic policy approach is required to deal with the "new" poverty as compared to the "old." In this sense, it provides a potentially testable set of hypotheses. In all fairness, though, this is not the only view that might be taken of contemporary poverty in the United States. The most obvious point at which a divergence might develop is in the area of defining poverty. Thus far, an absolute level of income definition has been suggested. Conceptually, this is not a clearly obvious way of defining poverty. However, it does have the advantage of permitting systemization of the various statements about the nature of the poverty problem that abounded in the early 1960's. But, there are alternatives. For example, Galbraith himself notes: "It is wrong to rest everything on absolutes. People are poverty stricken when their income, even if adequate for survival, falls markedly behind that of the community."[8] This rather clearly suggests a relativistic definition of poverty, i.e., gearing the poverty definition to the general standard of living in the society.

Historically, there have been a number of attempts at defining a minimum subsistence level of income—which is merely another way of measuring poverty. These appear to reflect the relativistic approach to poverty definition. Table 2 presents a summary of several such estimates for the United States during the twentieth century.[9] Clearly, through time, the concept of what constitutes a minimum subsistence level of income has advanced along with growth in the general level of

Table 2

ESTIMATES OF MINIMUM SUBSISTENCE LEVEL OF INCOME, UNITED STATES, 1905-1960, IN 1960 DOLLARS

Year	Family Minimum Subsistence Income
1905	$1,386
1910	1,434
1915	1,809
1920	1,665
1925	1,844
1930	2,015
1935	1,682
1940	1,765
1945	2,463
1950	2,378
1955	2,701
1960	2,662

per-capita income. This should not be unexpected. Poverty is a relative notion. People compare their living conditions with those around them and act accordingly. However, if we grant that poverty is a relative concept, what does that do to the argument that contemporary American poverty is something distinctly different from previous poverty? Simple: It plays havoc with it. In the extreme, the relativistic notion of poverty might suggest that the poverty level of income is some constant fraction of average income. If such were the case, the relative amount of poverty over time would change only if the basic distribution of family income was altered. Specifically, in order for poverty to become an isolated phenomenon rather than a majority one, the distribution of income would have had to shift dramatically in the direction of greater equality of income. While there may be some evidence to suggest that the pattern of income distribution in the United States has become more equal with the passage of time,[10] no serious student of income distribution would argue that the shift has been dramatic enough to account for the extreme decline in poverty that is implied by the hypothesis that contemporary poverty differs from historical poverty, assuming, of course, a relativistic definition of what constitutes poverty.

Actually, the relative approach to defining poverty, in combination with the notion that the modern poor are isolated from the mainstream of economic activity, implies just the opposite kind of shift in the pattern of income distribution, i.e., a movement towards a more unequal distribution. This can be seen by examining Figure 1. In that diagram, a hypothetical income distribution is shown (labeled A). Now, if, as economic growth occurs, those at the lower end of the income distribution are relatively unaffected, the distribution shifts in a fashion that "stretches" it out and the degree of inequality is increased. Such a shift is indicated by the distribution labeled B. Of course, accompanying the shift in the income distribution is a movement of the poverty boundary from P_1 to P_2. As drawn in Figure 1, this implies an increase in the poverty rate as economic growth occurs.

At this point, it becomes clear that a relativistic approach to defining poverty raises certain problems from the standpoint of its consistency with the basic hypotheses (1) that modern poverty differs from previous poverty and (2) that today's poor are relatively isolated from the mainstream of economic activity. In order for these hypotheses to be substantiated, there should be some evidence of an historical decline of fairly substantial proportions in the degree of inequality of income distribution followed by a recent tendency towards the reverse. As suggested earlier, this is a most unlikely sequence of events (more will be said about this in a later portion of the book). That does not mean that a relative view of poverty is inappropriate. However, it indicates the real possibility that it is inconsistent with certain of the characterizations of contemporary poverty that are so abundant.

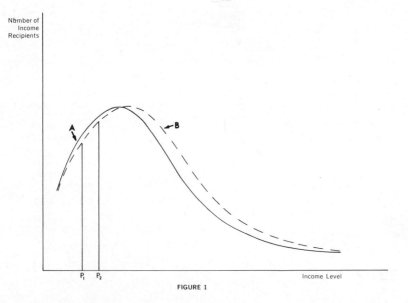

FIGURE 1

III. SOME SPECIFIC DEFINITIONS

We have dealt till now with definitions of poverty in a broad con-
ceptual manner without discussing in depth or detail the actual
mechanics of defining something called poverty. Let us look first at the
absolute approaches. When poverty emerged as a major issue in the
1960's, a first critical question was how to define it. The great bulk of
the discussion at that point focused on the particular choice of a level of
income that would indicate the presence of poverty. The argument was
intense with suggestions ranging from less than $2,000 per family to as
much as $5,000 per family. Some consensus did emerge around the
$3,000 of family income figure used earlier. While this was useful from
the standpoint of directing attention to the issue and permitting
comparisons of poverty levels through time, some rather obvious
shortcomings exist in such a simple straightforward technique for
defining poverty. An excellent brief statement of some of these
shortcomings is provided by Mollie Orshansky:[11]

> When the Council of Economic Advisors used annual income of
> less than $3,000 to define families living in poverty, it noted that
> this was a crude and approximate measure. Obviously the
> amount of cash income required to maintain any given level of
> living will be different for the family of two and the family of
> eight, for the person living in a large metropolitan area and a
> person of the same age and sex living on a farm.

In an effort to correct for the specific deficiencies mentioned in the
quoted statement, Miss Orshansky constructed a set of definitions of

poverty which takes into account differences in family size and whether a family is farm or non-farm. The basic technique she used to construct her definitions consists of calculating the amount of money income needed by a family to provide itself with a diet judged to be minimally adequate in a nutritional sense. Estimates of the cost per person of such a diet are available from the United States Department of Agriculture.[12] On the basis of those estimates, the amount of expenditures required for a minimally acceptable diet for families of various size can be calculated. In addition, it is possible to adjust the expenditures estimate to reflect the family's living on a farm and having access to food stuffs that are home grown.

Food, though, is only one aspect of a family's standard of living, albeit a crucial one. To take account of other types of expenditures in constructing a definition of poverty, Miss Orshansky then assumed (based on survey data) that non-food expenditures are twice as large as those for food. With such an assumption, it is then possible to extrapolate from the estimates of food expenditures and calculate the income levels that will permit the necessary amount of expenditures for food. Using this technique, she calculated that, for a non-farm family of four, an annual income level below $3,130 would be indicative of poverty. For a farm family of the same size, $1,860 was the poverty boundary. These estimates are for the year 1964 and are generally consistent with the $3,000 per family definition employed by the Council of Economic Advisors. In fact, the Orshansky definitions produce overall estimates of poverty that are quite similar to those obtained using the flat $3,000 per year per family standard. However, they are conceptually superior and have become the basis for the official poverty estimates disseminated by the Federal Government. For certain analytical purposes, they do present a problem, though. Whenever we wish to compare existing levels of poverty with those that prevailed prior to the early 1960's, we do not have estimates that are strictly comparable. Therefore, for many purposes, we will rely on poverty standards such as the $3,000 per family type since they permit accurate comparisons over longer periods of time.

One final word about the existing absolute definitions of poverty. The present official standards involve a substantial value judgment as to what is an adequate level of income. As such, they are subject to debate and they have been debated. Many feel that they set the poverty level of income at too low a point while some argue that they are too high.[13] For the purposes of this book, we need not defend or criticize the adequacy of the present definitions from the standpoint of their "justness." The great bulk of our discussion will deal with comparisons of poverty, either cross-sectionally or inter-temporally. For that purpose, what we require is definitions that are consistent although not necessarily "just." However, they shouldn't be too far off the mark on this last point. At the least, they should indicate low income status even though they may not identify poverty as precisely as we might like. The existing standards would certainly seem to do that.

Our present official poverty definitions have been with us for several years, years that have been marked by substantial economic growth. Consequently, the current poverty standard represents a substantially smaller fraction of average income in the United States than it did at its inception. Roughly, when first developed, the poverty boundary was set at about 50 percent of the median level of family income. Currently, it stands at about 40 percent of median family income. The drift downwards in the official poverty boundary relative to the general level of income has had the effect of raising serious questions concerning the validity of the present standards. Suggestions for upward revision are not uncommon with the basic justification usually being that as general levels of income rise the concept of what is a poverty level of economic well-being also changes. Victor Fuchs states:[14]

> As our nation prospers, our judgment as to what constitutes poverty will inevitably change. When we talk about poverty in America, we are talking about families and individuals who have much less income than most of us.

This is clearly a plea for a relative definition of poverty. There are two ways in which it could be implemented. The first would be through retention of our absolute definition of poverty with periodic upward revisions. One suspects that as the poverty boundary approaches some critical fraction of median income (I would estimate about one-third) the pressure for change in the standard will become sufficiently intense to force an upward shift. This would probably be to a level of income somewhere in the vicinity of about one-half the existing median level of income. Such a definition would yield a poverty rate of about 20 percent as compared to the eight to ten percent rate that would be associated with a poverty standard set at about one-third the median level of income. There are two basic reasons for expecting upward revisions in an absolute poverty standard from time to time. First, as the poverty boundary becomes a smaller fraction of the general level of income, it increasingly becomes suspect from the standpoint of its "fairness." Second, at the same time the official poverty rate will be declining and as it approaches some critical level, its very smallness will constitute a threat to the existence of a bureaucracy that is committed to fighting poverty. After all, a too successful fight to eliminate poverty may suggest that the bureaucracy itself is redundant. Since that same bureaucracy is in charge of the poverty definition, it will be in its own interest to change it. Consequently, if we persist in an absolute definition of poverty, what we can expect in the future is for the official poverty estimate to fluctuate between about eight and 20 percent as the definition of poverty is periodically changed.

There is an alternative approach to implementing a relative definition of poverty. It is to automatically escalate the poverty boundary as the general level of income rises. The most specific proposal along these lines has been suggested by Fuchs who argues for setting the poverty

Table 3

PERCENTAGE OF FAMILIES IN POVERTY WHEN POVERTY LEVEL OF INCOME IS DEFINED AS INCOME LESS THAN ONE-HALF THE MEDIAN, UNITED STATES, 1947-1970

Year	Percent of Families in Poverty
1947	18.9%
1948	19.1
1949	20.2
1950	20.0
1951	18.9
1952	18.9
1953	19.8
1954	20.9
1955	20.0
1956	19.6
1957	19.7
1958	19.8
1959	20.0
1960	20.3
1961	20.3
1962	19.8
1963	19.9
1964	19.9
1965	20.0
1966	19.2
1967	18.5
1968	18.3
1969	18.5
1970	19.0

Source: Department of Commerce, U.S. Bureau of the Census, *Current Population Reports*, P-60 Series (Washington, D.C.: U.S.G.P.O., various years).

standard at one-half the median level of income for the economy as a whole. The impact of such a proposal on the behavior of the aggregate poverty rate is shown by the data of Table 3. Those data show estimates of the percentage of families with poverty levels of income based on Fuch's criterion. Clearly, the effect of employing such a measure of poverty is to produce a roughly constant poverty rate, one varying between about 18 and 20 percent. This is exactly what one would expect unless there had been a substantial change in the overall pattern of income distribution in the United States.

While on the subject of poverty definitions that automatically escalate, we should take note of some recent contributions to the poverty and income distribution literature that suggest a definition of poverty that is relativistic in nature, but quite different from the definitions discussed so far. In a study prepared for the Joint Economic Committee of the Congress of the United States, great emphasis has been placed on the widening of the dollar gap (*not* the percentage difference) between the average income of those at the bottom and the top of the income distribution in the United States.[15] The drift of the argument is that such widening indicates a worsening of the economic status of the poor. Implicitly, this suggests that an appropriate way to define a poverty level of income is to focus on the absolute differential in dollars between the income of the poor and average income in the country. This I call an absolute gap approach to defining poverty. Using it, the poverty boundary can be defined as the median level of income minus some predetermined absolute dollar amount. This method of defining poverty will be discussed in much greater detail in a later chapter. For now, we simply note the existence of this alternative definition, although a warning is in order to the effect that it leads to some very strange conclusions.

IV. SOME SUMMARY COMMENTS

Enough has now been said to permit some sketchy and tentative remarks about the manner in which we perceive the poverty problem and the implications of alternative views of poverty. Essentially, there are two basic approaches to the poverty problem. One focuses on the backwash phenomenon and emphasizes the possibility that there are significant numbers of people in the United States who are so remotely associated with the normal workings of the economy that they cannot be assisted out of poverty through stimulating the general level of economic activity. This is a fascinating and important hypothesis that merits serious inquiry. If it is a valid contention, the public policy implications are substantial. Therefore, one of our major objectives in the remainder of this book will be the testing of this hypothesis. How we approach the testing process will depend on the way in which we choose to define poverty. The backwash thesis implies one thing if we are defining poverty in absolute terms and something quite different if a relative definition is used. This somewhat complicates the process of analysis but not sufficiently to prohibit it.

The second broad view of poverty perceives it as purely a problem of the degree of inequality of the pattern of income distribution. This approach does not depend on the existence of a backwash phenomenon in order to argue that poverty is a serious problem. As clear and direct a statement of this position is Fuchs' comment, "When we talk about reducing or eliminating poverty, we are really talking about changing the distribution of income. . ."[16] This is a much broader and more sweeping view of the nature of the poverty problem than that embodied in the backwash approach, largely because any attempt to eliminate poverty as thus conceived must perforce deal with the factors that determine the incomes of all persons rather than just those that affect the incomes of the group defined as being poor. In short, it implies working with the entire income distribution instead of a relatively small portion of it. Further, such a view of the poverty problem has entirely different social implications. It suggests a much more fundamental shortcoming in our social and economic institutions than does the backwash concept. Basically, it questions the entire system of income distribution in the United States; not just whether everyone has an opportunity to participate in that system. Therefore, as far as possible, it is desirable that we also explore and examine this view of poverty, for it may well be the more important one.

In order to complete our broad overview and perspective of poverty in America, a few words should be said about poverty in the United States compared to other parts of the world. Table 4 shows per capita income levels for a number of countries including the United States. Assuming that in the United States we set the poverty level of income at about one-half the average (as we did in the early 1960's), it is clear that what we call a poverty level of income is well above the average in most of the remainder of the world and only rarely below the average, even among other "developed" economies. In a sense, it may seem almost pretentious for the United States to set poverty levels of income that would represent pure luxury for the majority of the world's population. It is somewhat akin to the "rich kid on the block" talking about how poor he is compared to his relatives and friends. Yet, it is defensible in some ways for it reflects the essential uniqueness of the American experience, namely, unprecedented wealth and income and the problems that accompany it. In a way, our seeming preoccupation with the poverty issue may signify nothing more than our own discomfort at being so far ahead of the great bulk of the world in terms of living standards. In fact, the difference between income levels in the United States and the remainder of the world is so pronounced that a good case can be made for claiming that relative to the world as a whole, poverty in the United States is a special phenomenon restricted to a small

Table 4

GROSS NATIONAL PRODUCT PER CAPITA,
VARIOUS COUNTRIES, 1969

Country	Per Capita Income	Country	Per Capita Income
United States	$4,240	Lebanon	$ 580
Sweden	2,920	Mexico	580
Switzerland	2,700	Yugoslavia `	580
Canada	2,650	Uruguay	560
France	2,460	Chile	510
Denmark	2,310	Portugal	510
Australia	2,300	Albania	430
New Zealand	2,230	Iran	350
West Germany	2,190	Turkey	350
Norway	2,160	Malaysia	340
Belgium	2,010	Peru	330
Finland	1,980	Iraq	310
United Kingdom	1,890	Taiwan	300
Netherlands	1,760	Colombia	290
East Germany	1,570	Zambia	290
Israel	1,570	Cuba	280
Austria	1,470	Dominican Rep.	280
Japan	1,430	Jordan	280
Italy	1,400	North Korea	280
Czechoslovakia	1,370	Brazil	270
USSR	1,200	Syria	260
Hungary	1,100	Rhodesia	240
Argentina	1,060	South Korea	210
Venezuela	1,000	Phillipines	210
Poland	890	Bolivia	160
Bulgaria	860	South Vietnam	140
Romania	860	India	110
Greece	840	Indonesia	100
Spain	820	China	Less
South Africa	710	Nigeria	than
Panama	660	North Vietnam	$100

Source: *Finance and Development,* International Monetary Fund and
World Bank Group, No. 1, 1972, p. 51.

proportion of the population. Certainly, when contrasted with the underdeveloped nations of the world where famine and starvation are frequently very real threats for the majority of the people, American poverty is a distinctly different animal. In this context, the often made contention that contemporary American poverty is unique has validity. However, this is not the sense in which that claim is usually advanced.

With these various reflections on the nature of the poverty problem as background, we are now in a position to proceed with a more detailed discussion of the economic aspects of poverty. As a first step, the next two chapters will be devoted to an in-depth treatment of the factors that determine the income levels of people within the framework of a relatively free market economy. This will provide a basis for evaluating the determinants of poverty in the United States. Following this, a series of chapters will be devoted to (1) exploring the validity of the backwash proposition in general, (2) examining the extent to which poverty in the United States is inherited from generation to generation, (3) describing the nature and causes of poverty among various population sub-groups (non-whites, the aged, and females), (4) a discussion of regional differences in poverty, and (5) a summary statement of conclusions and the policy prescriptions they suggest. The end result will hopefully be a more informed view of the economic dimensions of poverty in the United States.

FOOTNOTES

[1] J.K. Galbraith, *The Affluent Society*, Boston: Houghton Mifflin Co., 1958, pp. 323-333.

[2] For example, this is the general theme of Oscar Ornati, *Poverty Amid Affluence: A Report on a Research Project*. New York: The New school for Social Research, The Twentieth Century Fund, 1966.

[3] We will focus in this book on an income level definition of poverty. Arguments can be made for definitions based on considerations other than income. For example, see S.M. Miller, Martin Rein, Pamela Roby, and Bertram M. Gross, "Poverty, Inequality, and Conflict," *The Annals of the American Academy of Political and Social Science*, September 1967, pp. 18-52. In this piece, it is maintained that some type of "social indicators" definition of poverty is desirable. For our purposes, though, we will abide by an income definition.

[4] These definitions are based on the work done by Mollie Orshansky of the Social Security Administration. See "Counting the Poor: Another Look at the Poverty Profile," *Social Security Bulletin*. January 1965, pp. 3-13.

[5]The source of these data is *Historical Statistics of the United States, Colonial Times to 1957.* Washington, D.C.: United States Department of Commerce, Bureau of the Census, 1960, Series G 99-117, p. 166.

[6] Again, see Galbraith, *op. cit.* In addition, one of the most influential works arguing along these lines was Michael Harrington, *The Other America: Poverty in the United States.* Baltimore: Penguin Books, 1964.

[7]"The Problem of Poverty in America," in *Economic Report of the President,* January 1964, p. 72.

[8] Galbraith, *op. cit.,* p. 323.

[9] These are taken from Ornati, *op. cit.,* pp. 149-150.

[10]The most consistent evidence of a trend toward greater equality is presented in Lee Soltow, "Economic Inequality in the United States in the Period from 1790 to 1860," *Journal of Economic History,* December 1971, pp. 822-839 and "Evidence on Income Inequality in the United States, 1866-1965," *Journal of Economic History,* June 1969, pp. 279-286. For other evidence that is consistent with Soltow's conclusions, see Simon Kuznets, *Shares of Upper Income Groups in Income and Savings.* New York: National Bureau of Economic Research, 1953.

[11]Orshanky, *op. cit.,* p. 3.

[12]See *Family Food Plans and Food Costs.* Washington, D.C.: United States Department of Agriculture, November 1962, Home Economics Research Report No. 20.

[13]For a critique of the existing poverty definitions, see Rose Friedman, *Poverty: Definition and Perspective.* Washington, D.C.: American Enterprise Institute for Public Policy Research, 1965, particularly pp. 2-42.

[14]Victor Fuchs, "Redefining Poverty and Redistributing Income," *The Public Interest,* Summer 1967, p. 91.

[15]The study is entitled "The American Distribution of Income: A Structural Problem." It was prepared by Lester Thurow and Robert Lucas for the Joint Economic Committee.

[16]Fuchs, *op. cit.,* p. 91.

PERSONAL INCOME IN A MARKET ECONOMY

From the drift of the argument of the preceding chapter, it is apparent that any meaningful discussion of poverty must focus on the determinants of the distribution of income in the United States. An appropriate framework for that discussion is provided by the economic theory of how income is distributed in a free market economy, which is essentially what the United States is. For the most part, formal economic theory emphasizes what is thought of as the "functional" distribution of income, i.e., the way in which income is allocated among the various broad classes of productive factors. In the simplest formulation, two types of productive factors might be considered, labor and capital. The prices of these inputs into the productive process are critical in determining the distribution of income among them, and these prices, in turn, reflect the demand for and supply of the productive factors in question. In a competitive economy, the quantities demanded and supplied of each of the factors of production will be equated at a set of equilibrium prices and the distribution of income determined.

The concept of the functional distribution of income has received substantial attention because it has important implications from the standpoint of social justice. In a world in which the ideas of Karl Marx are more than mere historical curiosities, the division of an economy's output between the owners of human and non-human productive services can be an exceedingly emotional issue. The literature surrounding the subject is wide and deals extensively with the question of variations in the share of national income that accrues to the different factors of production. Of particular interest is the behavior of the labor share of income. Changes in the labor share of private income in the United States are shown by the data of Table 1 for the period 1929 to present. The maximum proportion is 70.2 percent in 1933, while the minimum is 56.1 in 1929.[1] This is a fairly wide range of variation and certainly belies a frequently advanced hypothesis of constancy in labor's share of national income.[2]

I. THE RELATIONSHIP BETWEEN FUNCTIONAL AND PERSONAL INCOME DISTRIBUTION

While the data describing the functional distribution of income in the United States are interesting and informative, their relationship to the problem of poverty as it was treated in Chapter One may not be obvious. There, our interest was in the personal distribution of income rather than in the functional. The personal distribution of income differs from the functional by focusing on the individual recipient of income instead of grouping the receivers of income according to the type of productive service they sell in the markets for the factors of

Table 1

LABOR SHARE OF PRIVATE INCOME
IN THE UNITED STATES, 1929-1968

Year	Labor Share* as Percent of Private Income	Year	Labor Share* as Percent of Private Income
1929	56.1	1949	61.6
1930	59.6	1950	60.8
1931	63.9	1951	61.2
1932	70.0	1952	63.1
1933	70.2	1953	64.8
1934	66.1	1954	65.7
1935	61.3	1955	65.2
1936	61.6	1956	65.5
1937	61.3	1957	66.3
1938	62.2	1958	66.1
1939	61.9	1959	65.8
1940	59.8	1960	66.9
1941	57.8	1961	67.5
1942	57.0	1962	67.5
1943	57.8	1963	67.8
1944	59.0	1964	65.9
1945	60.0	1965	64.9
1946	60.8	1966	65.2
1947	62.0	1967	66.4
1948	60.4	1968	66.7

Source: U.S. Department of Commerce.

* Labor income is defined as total compensation of employees.

production. To fully grasp the linkage between the two types of income distribution, it is important to keep in mind that our primary interest is in the degree of inequality in the personal income distribution and changes in the magnitude of inequality through time. Inequality in the personal distribution of income can occur within the context of a competitive market economy if there is inequality in the distribution of ownership of the factors of production. One possibility in this respect is inequality in the distribution of claims to the non-human (or property) type inputs used in the production of goods and services. There is clear evidence of substantial inequality in the distribution of property (or wealth) as shown in Table 2. The simplest measure of the degree of inequality implicit in a distribution such as that shown in Table 2 is the Gini coefficient which may range in value from zero (indicating perfect equality in a distribution) to one (which means perfect inequality).[3] The Gini coefficient for the distribution of Table 2 is .756 , which suggests substantial inequality. To the extent, then, that receipt of income is dependent on the sale of productive services of a property type, inequality will be introduced into the personal income distribution.

Table 2

CUMULATIVE DISTRIBUTION OF WEALTH*
IN THE UNITED STATES, 1962

	Amount of Wealth	Percent of Individuals	Percent of Total Wealth
	$ 0	8.1	- 0.2
	1,000	25.4	0.0
	5,000	42.7	2.1
	10,000	56.9	6.6
Less	25,000	81.3	23.8
Than	50,000	92.5	40.9
	100,000	97.6	55.9
	200,000	98.6	61.3
	500,000	99.5	74.2
	0 to 500,000 and over	100.0	100.0

Source: *Federal Reserve Bulletin*, "Survey of Financial Characteristics," March 1964, p. 291.

* Wealth is defined as net worth.

Consequently, the relative importance of income derived from the ownership of property is a crucial determinant of the degree of inequality of personal income distribution.

The data of Table 1 suggest that approximately one-third of income in the American economy is derived from property sources. However, this may be somewhat misleading since these data are confined to income generated in the private sector of the economy. This excludes substantial sources of income that enter into the determination of the personal income distribution of the United States. For example, wages and salaries paid to government employees and government transfer payments are excluded[4] Table 3 shows the basic elements of personal income in the United States for the third quarter of 1971 expressed as annual rates of flow. The major component is compensation of employees ($645.6 billion), which includes all wages and salaries and supplements to wages and salaries in both the private and public sectors. Actually, not all of this total enters into the aggregate personal income statistic. Certain of the supplements to wages and salaries, contributions for Social Security, are deducted. These amount to $65.4 billion which reduces the compensation of employees component to $580.2 billion. This income flow rather clearly derives from the sale of productive services of a human type. Thus, none of it is assigned to the property income category.

Table 3

COMPONENTS OF PERSONAL INCOME, UNITED STATES, THIRD QUARTER, 1971

Type of Income	Amount of Income ($ billions)
Wages and Salaries	580.2
Proprietorships and Partnerships	69.2
Rental Income	24.5
Dividends	19.2
Net Interest	42.4
Government Transfer Payments	92.5
Total	828.0

Source: U.S. Department of Commerce.

The second largest flow of personal income (other than transfer payments) is that accruing to individual proprietors, $69.2 billion. Whether this income is the result of the sale of human or non-human resources is not clearly evident. Proprietor's income consists of a "mixed bag" of income streams, some of which derive from the ownership of property and some of which represent a return to the human services (or labor) supplied by the individual proprietor. In an opportunity cost sense, the individual proprietor, say the local owner of a family grocery store, should view the wage income he could earn in an alternative employment as a cost of doing business. Thus, a part of his total income stream is really that opportunity cost "wage" and should be viewed as resulting from the sale of his human resources. The exact proportion of proprietor's income that should be assigned to the human resource component is difficult to estimate, but we will assume that an equal division between the human and non-human components is appropriate. This would result in assigning $34.6 billion to the income derived from the sale of human resources and an equal amount to income received from property sources.

Three of the remaining components of personal income are rather easily classified, namely interest, rental, and dividend income. Clearly, these result from the sale of the productive services of non-human or property resources. Collectively, they total $86.1 billion of income which, combined with the $34.6 billion of proprietor's income assigned to the property category, gives $120.7 billion of income derived from property sources.[5]

The only remaining element of personal income is transfer payments. These total $92.5 billion and present some problems from the standpoint of allocating them between the property and non-property categories. In one sense, the transfers do not represent a sale of any type of economic resources; for example, unemployment compensation benefits or general assistance payments.[6] However, a major portion of the transfers are Social Security payments, particularly old age retirement benefits. Theoretically, these have been financed by prior contributions to the Social Security Trust Fund. Thus, they should represent the same type of return as that produced by an insurance policy or an annuity. In this sense, the income stream that is recorded is partly interest income derived from the Trust Fund's ownership of securities and partly merely the consumption of past saving. This would suggest attributing this income stream to the property income classification. In reality, though, this is an unrealistic view of the American Social Security System. When initially created, it was supposedly to function on the same actuarial principles as a private insurance company. Basically, that means the administrators of the system would have to have on hand at all times assets sufficient to satisfy all outstanding obligations, i.e., they could not rely on a future stream of payments into the Social Security Trust Fund to meet preceding obligations.

A brief appraisal of the present size of the Social Security Trust Fund indicates clearly that it is not sufficient to meet outstanding obligations.[7] In effect, financing of future obligations will be funded by relying on current receipts from the wage tax that is a part of the Social Security legislation. Consequently, it is appropriate to think of this income flow as resulting from a transfer of wage income from one part of the population to another. Thus, it may properly be regarded as being generated from the sale of human resources. The remainder of the transfer payment category probably best belongs in the human resource income classification also. For the most part, it is simply the result of someone being able to establish a basic claim to income on the grounds of his existence as a human being; the best example of this

Table 4

DISTRIBUTION OF WAGE AND SALARY
INCOME AMONG MALES WITH
SUCH INCOME, 1970

Income Class	Percent in Class
$ 1 — 499	7.4
500 — 999	4.8
1000 — 1499	3.5
1500 — 1999	2.9
2000 — 2499	2.7
2500 — 2999	2.0
3000 — 3999	5.2
4000 — 4999	5.8
5000 — 5999	6.9
6000 — 6999	7.8
7000 — 7999	8.8
8000 — 9999	15.0
10000 — 14999	19.0
15000 — 24999	6.6
25000 and over	1.6

Source: U.S. Bureau of the Census, Current Population Survey.

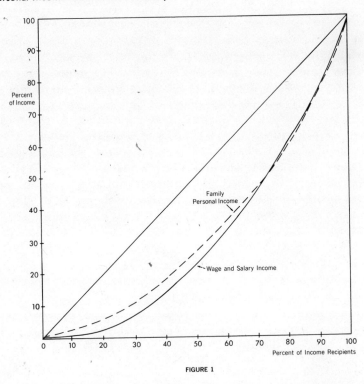

FIGURE 1

being general assistance or welfare payments. Therefore, we will regard the entire transfer payment income component of personal income as being human resource type income.

Summing the various personal income components into the broad categories of property and non-property income reveals that of $828.0 billion of income, $120.7 billion, or 14.58 percent, was derived from property sources. This is about one-seventh of the total. Therefore, it is obvious that the major source of inequality in the personal income distribution must lie in inequality in the distribution of ownership of human resources. To remove any doubt on this point, simply examine Table 4 and Figure 1. Table 4 shows the distribution of wage and salary income among males with such income in 1970 and the solid line of Figure 1 depicts the Lorenz curve associated with that distribution. The Gini coefficient for that distribution is .379. For comparison purposes, the Lorenz curve for the entire 1970 distribution of personal income by families and unrelated individuals is shown by the dotted line of Figure 1. It shows a more equal distribution (Gini coefficient of .333) than that for wage and salary income. Consequently, any explanation of the basic inequality of personal income distribution in the United States must account for the inequality in the distribution of wage and salary income.[8]

II. INEQUALITY IN OWNERSHIP OF HUMAN RESOURCES

The notion of inequality in the distribution of ownership of human resources is an interesting one. How could this happen in a world in which true slavery does not exist? After all, the only human resource an individual can own is himself. This would seem to suggest relative equality in the distribution of ownership of human resources. This is true if by human resources we mean something that can be thought of as homogeneous "pure labor." However, this type of productive factor only exists in the assumptions of formal economic models. In reality, pure labor is combined with elements of what is popularly called "human capital."[9] Conceptually, it is frequently useful to think of human capital as a separate factor of production that enters independently into the economist's concept of a production function.[10] If human capital is treated in this fashion, the income stream accruing to an individual who sells his labor services becomes a composite of a return to pure labor and a return to human capital. Further, it is quite possible for inequality in the ownership of human capital to exist in our society.

Disparities in the quantity of human capital possessed by different individuals can arise for two basic reasons. Human capital can be thought of as being either of an inherited or an acquired form. By inherited human capital, we mean the "genetic package" that each of us receives as an accident of birth. Because of variations in that "package", each of us has a comparative advantage in the performance of certain types of tasks.[11] Consequently, given a certain structure of demand in the society for the performance of various types of activities, relative scarcities of the specific ability to perform these tasks develop. With them come differential returns to these abilities which, in turn, produce inequalities in the distribution of income derived from the sale of human resources. To illustrate this, let us take an example. In a society that generates a substantial demand for entertainment through the medium of games such as football, baseball, basketball, etc.,[12] the genetic accident of having the specific physical skills to play these games will generate for the individual fortunate enough to have these skills a marked advantage in terms of his position in the overall income distribution. Henry Aaron (the baseball player, not the economist), as a case in point, is capable of commanding an annual income of $200,000 by selling his services as a baseball player. This places him in the extreme upper tail of the income distribution, primarily because of chance. Aaron's position in the income distribution is doubly a matter of chance. On the one hand, there is the matter of his having those specific skills required to hit a baseball thrown at a small area from a distance of 60 feet, six inches at speeds of as much as 100 miles per hour. In addition, he is also a beneficiary of chance phenomena by being fortunate enough to live at a time when the general population is sufficiently interested in baseball to support it (either directly or indirectly) in a manner that will permit the payment of Aaron's $200,000 a year salary. The end result is great disparities in the economic returns to inherited abilities and an introduction of an element of inequality into the personal income distribution.

In addition to differentials in the genetic endowment of individuals with elements of human capital, there may also exist disparities in the ownership of non-inherited components of human capital. These are the variants of human capital that develop from either (1) the accidents of an individual's postnatal environment and/or (2) a conscious effort by individuals or society to modify the distribution of ownership of human capital. The first of these is exemplified by the impact on an individual of differences in his physical and social environment that are largely outside his control while the second is perhaps best illustrated by the phenomenon of investment in education at various levels. Clearly, either of these forms of non-genetic human capital may be distributed in an unequal fashion in our society. Substantial differences in individual environments at birth do exist and, despite the educational revolution of the post-World War II period, great differentials in individual holdings of educational human capital are still found. Consequently, variations in the pattern of ownership of acquired human capital resources may contribute substantially to the existence of inequalities in the personal income distribution.

Another source of differentials in the distribution of human resource income is transfer payment income. As already suggested, individuals can exercise a claim on income by the very fact of their existence. This can be thought of as the "social right" aspect of income derived from human resources. Income obtained from this source takes the form of outright transfers of income within the system that do not ultimately derive from some prior sale of human resources. In fact, the ability to exercise a "social right" claim is for the most part inversely related to an individual's previous history of selling and present ability to sell human resources in return for income. Consequently, this form of return to human resources undoubtedly has the effect of counterbalancing inequalities in income distribution that result from differentials in the ownership of the various components of human capital.

The critical question at this point is the relative importance of the various sources of non-property income in producing inequalities in income distribution. Clearly, the non-social-right components are the strongest contributors to inequality with the human capital factors (as distinguished from the "pure" labor element) probably being the most dominant. Of the two types of human capital, the acquired is perhaps the most interesting because of its potential for control from the policy standpoint. On the other hand, the inherited differences in human capital may well be the most important from the standpoint of producing income inequalities.

III. INSTITUTIONAL SOURCES OF INCOME INEQUALITY

One other aspect of income inequality remains. All that has been said till now is within the general framework of a highly competitive free market economy. At no time have we dealt with the possibility of imperfections in market mechanisms that might contribute to creating more or less inequality in the personal income distribution. A number of possibilities suggest themselves in this respect. First, what about the possible impact of monopsony power in the hands of the employers of productive services. In particular, consider the trade unionist vision of the monopsonistic employer forcing extremely low wage rates on helpless (meaning unorganized) employees. To the extent that this does occur, its major impact on the personal income distribution would be through its effect on the pattern of functional distribution of income. Employer monopsony means that workers are paid less than their marginal product and the non-labor share of total income is inflated. This is the classic case of economic exploitation of employees and it produces inequalities in the personal income distribution by shifting income from wage earners to property holders.

On the other hand, there is the opposite argument to the effect that trade unions possess substantial amounts of monoply power in the labor market which permits them to alter the income distribution in their favor. The presence of this type of market power probably would have its greatest impact directly on the personal income distribution. At least, economic theory suggests that the possession of monopoly power by trade unions would have little impact on the functional distribution of income as long as employers remain free to adjust the quantity demanded of labor.[13] Under such conditions they presumably would employ the quantity of labor that would equate the marginal productivity of labor with the wage rate.[14] However, trade union monopoly power could conceivably have a strong impact within the personal income distribution by redistributing income from the non-unionized portion of the labor force to the unionized.

Discrimination against sub-groups of the labor force is another potential source of income inequality that may be attributed to market imperfections. If we interpret discrimination as being the result of employers' experiencing subjective costs when they hire minority group workers,[15] discrimination results in a decrease in the minority worker's marginal productivity and presumably will have a two-edged effect on income distribution. First, there will be some shift in the functional distribution of income in favor of property income in order for employers to be compensated for the subjective costs they experience when hiring minority group workers. Second, since the burden of the change in the functional distribution of income is borne entirely by minority group workers, there will be a change in the personal distribution of income. Given minority group workers' low income status, the change is obviously in the direction of producing greater inequality in the personal income distribution.

Finally, the degree of inequality in the personal income distribution may be affected by legislation that inhibits the normal working of the labor market. An example of this type of legislation is minimum wage laws. Minimum wage laws have the avowed purpose of producing a more equal distribution of income through the setting of some minimum below which money wage rates may not fall. However, due to their employment effects it is indeed questionable whether they accomplish this objective, particularly since their employment effects fall most strongly on marginal labor force groups that are already low income.[16] Other direct legislative interferences with the system of income distribution can be documented, such as agricultural subsidies, tariffs and quotas to protect American industry, and licensing of occupations to protect the consumer interest.[17] Their net effect on the inequality of income distribution is debatable, but it is by no means obvious that they lead to greater equality of income distribution. It may well be that they have the opposite effect.

IV. CONCLUSIONS

The major conclusion suggested thus far in this chapter is that any adequate explanation of the existence of poverty in the United States must explain differences in the ownership of human resources in the system. It is not enough to deal in cliches to the effect that the owners of property are exploiting those who have to depend on the sale of their human resources in order to earn income. Fundamental disparities in the ability of individuals to command human resource income are apparent and these, as much as anything else, explain inequalities in income distribution. This suggests that the presence of poverty will be associated with those personal attributes that imply a limited ability to earn human resource income; for example, low education, limited genetic endowment, characteristics that give rise to discrimination, and/or lack of market power relative to other sub-groups of the population. This is essentially what is found in those studies that attempt to assess the causes of poverty. Thurow, for one, finds that poverty is associated with living on a farm, being non-white, having limited access to the labor market, and being poorly educated.[8] Simply what one would expect. Therefore, in the detailed treatment of the causes of poverty among various sub-groups we shall focus primarily on factors of this type as explanations of poverty.

FOOTNOTES

[1]These data have not been adjusted to take into consideration shifts in industrial composition over time.

[2]Perhaps the most perceptive article dealing with the constancy of relative shares hypothesis is Robert M. Solow, "A Skeptical Note on the Constancy of Relative Shares," *American Economic Review*, September 1958, pp. 618-631.

[3]The calculation of the Gini coefficient is illustrated by the diagram that follows. The curve A (known as a Lorenz Curve) describes the per-

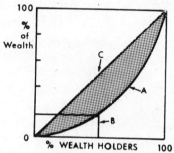

centages of total wealth (or income) held (or received) by various fractions of the wealth (or income) holding (or receiving) population, counting up from those with the least wealth. Thus, point B on the Lorenz Curve indicates that the bottom 50 percent of the population hold 20 percent of the total wealth. Now, the Gini coefficient is simply the ratio of the area lying between the Lorenz Curve and the diagonal line C (shaded in the diagram) to the area lying between C and the two axes of the diagram. Clearly, if wealth were distributed in a perfectly equal fashion, the Lorenz Curve and C would coincide and the Gini coefficient would be zero. Also, if one person held all the wealth, the Lorenz Curve and the axes of the diagram would coincide and the Gini coefficient would equal one.

[4]A transfer payment represents income for which one does not provide a productive service in exchange. Examples would be unemployment compensation or general assistance payments.

[5]One could argue that retained earnings of corporations also represent income derived from property. To the extent that these exist, they presumably are reflected in the prices of equity holdings in the various corporations. Thus, they become a part of wealth and are income in the sense of being capital gains. They are not included, though, in the personal income concept. However, their existence should be kept in mind and it should be realized that property income is somewhat greater than what is reported here.

[6]In one sense, unemployment compensation benefits can be regarded as being a payment for human resources that have previously been sold in the market. Eligibility for unemployment compensation generally presumes a prior employment history and, consequently, can be thought of as being "earned" through previous work.

[7]The Social Security Trust Fund totals about $30 billion as contrasted to obligations that approach $500 billion.

[8]While wage and salary income is not the only source of income derived from the ownership of human resources, it is clearly the major one.

[9]The term "human capital" was popularized by Theodore Schultz and Gary Becker. See Schultz, T.W., "Investment in Human Capital," *American Economic Review*, March 1961, pp. 1-17 and Becker, Gary S., *Human Capital*. New York: Columbia University Press, 1964.

[10]Statistical production functions that incorporate human capital as a separate and distinct factor of production have been estimated. See Scully, G.W., "Human Capital and Productivity in U.S. Manufacturing," *Western Economic Journal*, December 1969, pp. 334-340.

[11]The principle of comparative advantage is a familiar one to economists. Simply put, it holds that all that must exist in order for mutually advantageous specialization and trade to occur is differences in the *relative* efficiency with which various tasks are performed by different people.

[12]The demand for these forms of entertainment is reflected in either actual gate receipts or the revenue derived from the sale of radio and/or television rights to the performance.

[13]The possible impact of trade unions on the functional distribution of income is discussed rather thoroughly in N.J. Simler, *The Impact of Unionism on Wage-Income Ratios in the Manufacturing Sector of the Economy*. University of Minnesota Press, 1961.

[14]By marginal productivity we simply mean the value of the addition to output (net of *additional* non-wage costs incurred in its production) generated by the last worker hired. If we assume homogeneous workers, every worker may be thought of as the last one hired.

[15]This is a concept pioneered by Gary Becker. See Becker, G.S., *The Economics of Discrimination*. University of Chicago Press, 1957.

[16]For evidence of this impact see, Adie, Douglas, and Chapin, Gene L., "Teenage Unemployment Experiences and Federal Minimum Wage Legislation," *Industrial Relations Research Association Proceedings*, 1970, pp. 117-127; Kosters, Marvin, and Welch, Finis, "The Effects of Minimum Wages on the Distribution of Changes in Aggregate Employment," *American Economic Review*, June 1972, pp. 323-332; and Moore, T.G., "The Effect of Minimum Wages on Employment," *Journal of Political Economy*, July/August 1971, pp. 897-902.

[17]Occupational licensing may not appear to represent legislative interference in the system of income distribution. However, the inevitable result of effective licensing is exclusion of certain individuals from the activity in question. This tends to produce higher incomes for those

fortunate enough (or skilled enough) to be licensed. Witness the case of physicians.

[18]Thurow, Lester C., "The Causes of Poverty," *Quarterly Journal of Economics*, February 1967, pp. 39-57.

THE PERSONAL DISTRI- BUTION OF INCOME: PAST AND PRESENT

Few questions in economics are more provocative than that of income distribution, probably because almost everyone feels affected by the pattern of income distribution in our society. Whatever one's position in life, the overall distribution of income is important since it provides a benchmark against which all of us can compare our economic status with that of others. If such a statement sounds somewhat crass and materialistic, so much the better. The intent in making it was to suggest the pervasiveness of concern for one's economic status that marks the world. How often do we encounter people with a substantial commitment to improving the lot of the underprivileged through income redistribution who are also striving as hard as they can to improve their own position in the income distribution even though they may already be very highly placed in that distribution. At almost any major institution of higher learning in the United States faculty members can be found who (1) are in the top quintile of the income distribution, (2) rail against the basic inequality of the income distribution, and (3) complain bitterly if their salary is not increased at a substantial rate each year.[1] The inconsistency of these positions is somewhat apparent. But, why would someone who presumably is so dedicated to logical thinking have such a set of views? The answer is relatively simple. Very few people are really aware of where their income places them in the income distribution. Academicians, for example, have been so attuned historically to pleading poverty that they actually believe their own protestations and simply assume that they are relatively poorly placed in the society's income distribution. In reality, they are as a rule quite favorably positioned.[2]

Others think similarly about their income position. In general, the notion of what constitutes being truly wealthy involves a standard of living available only to those at the extreme upper tail of the income distribution.[3] Consequently, few people, including the great bulk of those actually in the top quintile of the personal income distribution, perceive of themselves as being wealthy. Therefore, they can talk of the need for income redistribution from the top quintile to the bottom without realizing that they are members of the top quintile. They merely regard themselves as being part of the great middle of the income distribution that has to struggle to meet their budgetary commitments just like everyone else. To judge how easy it is for this to happen, examine the personal income distribution shown in Table 1. These data are for families and unrelated individuals for the year 1970

Table 1

DISTRIBUTION OF PERSONAL INCOME, FAMILIES AND UNRELATED INDIVIDUALS, UNITED STATES, 1970

Income Class	Percent in Class
Less than $3000	8.9
3000—4999	10.4
5000—6999	11.8
7000—9999	19.9
10000—14999	26.8
15000—24999	17.7
25000 and over	4.6

Source: U.S. Bureau of the Census, Current Population Survey

and show that the income boundary that defines the top quintile of the personal income distribution is slightly in excess of $16,000 per year.[4] This is not a level of income that most people would regard as sufficient to make someone wealthy. Going one step further, we find that less than five percent of the distribution has income in excess of $25,000 a year. This is certainly a magnificent sum as viewed from the bottom of the income distribution, but not nearly sufficient to support the stereotype living standard that most people associate with being truly wealthy. In short, while a number of families in the United States have relatively high incomes, very few would truly qualify as being wealthy, particularly if allowed to determine for themselves whether they should be placed in that category.

I. HISTORICAL PATTERNS OF INCOME DISTRIBUTION

If the previous discussion suggests the existence of myths concerning patterns of income distribution, again, so much the better. Any number of such myths exist beginning with some historical ones about the degree of equality of income distribution that once existed in the United States. It is interesting to speculate that at a time when the United States was essentially an agrarian society, the distribution of wealth and income in America was much more equal. Pursuing this reasoning further, one may also speculate that after this initial period of relative equality the process of industrialization of the United States operated to create greater inequality as wealth and property became more concentrated in the hands of the owners of capital. Certainly, such hypothesizing fits what Soltow recently called the "romantic" myth of an early age of unspoiled agrarian innocence.[5] This notion is not a new one. Rather, it finds early expression in the writings of both American and foreign commentators on American society. As straightforward a statement as any of this idea is Reynal's depiction of the American colonies as being characterized by "a certain equality of station, a security that arises from property."[6]

The truth of the matter appears to be that no such egalitarian agricultural society ever existed in the United States. Rather, there seems to be clear evidence that inequality in the measures of economic status that are available was greater in the early part of the nineteenth century than it was at the outbreak of the Civil War.[7] In fact, what is suggested is a general tendency towards a more equal distribution of wealth and income throughout the history of the United States. Admittedly, the data prior to World War I are less than perfect, but what there is appears to be consistent with this premise. For example, Soltow concludes "some very tenuous income tax data for 1894 certainly negate the idea that the level /of inequality/ was higher nearer the turn of the century than it was earlier or later."[8] Commencing with 1913, we have clearer evidence with respect to changes in the degree of inequality found in the distribution of income. Kuznets' classic study suggests little change between 1913 and 1929, but a substantial decrease in the share of income received by the top one and five percent of income recipients between 1929 and 1946 (see Table 2).[9] The shift after 1929 appears to have been the result of both structural changes that reduced the share of economic income accruing to the top of the income distribution and alterations in the tax structure that further reduced the share of top income recipients. For example, the top one percent of income recipients received 17.15 percent of all economic income in 1929 and only 9.58 percent in 1946. Further, in 1929, they claimed 18.92 percent of disposable income (more than their share of economic income) while, by 1946, this had been reduced to 7.71 percent (less than their share of economic income).

The great shift in income distribution between 1929 and 1946 has been generally attributed to the impact of the social and economic policies of the New Deal during the 1930's and the effect of World War II on the economy. However, following 1946, there has been a slowing of the rate of decrease in inequality of income distribution. In fact, the claim is frequently made that there has been no further decline in income inequality since the "great shift." The most recent example of such a claim is a study by Thurow and Lucas that advances the proposition that the shares of income accruing to the various quintiles

Table 2

SHARES OF TOTAL INCOME RECEIVED
BY TOP 1 PERCENT AND TOP 5 PERCENT
OF TOTAL POPULATION, UNITED STATES,
1913, 1929, and 1946

Year	Basic Income Variant*		Economic Income Variant*		Disposable Income Variant*	
	Top 1 Percent	Top 5 Percent	Top 1 Percent	Top 5 Percent	Top 1 Percent	Top 5 Percent
1913	14.98%	---%	---%	---%	---%	---%
1929**	14.50	26.09	---	---	---	---
1929***	14.65	26.36	17.31	32.19	19.08	33.81
1946	8.98	18.20	9.58	19.96	7.71	17.66

Source: **Historical Statistics of the United States, Colonial Times to 1957,** Series G-81-146.

*For definitions of the income variants, see the text discussion accompanying the data series in the basic source.

**Comparable with 1913.

***Comparable with 1946.

of the income distribution remained unchanged between 1947 and 1970.[10] This is an important finding but, unfortunately, the evidence simply does not support it. The shares of income for the various quintiles as well as the top five percent of income recipients for families over the years 1947 through 1970 are shown in Table 3. Observe in particular the data for 1947 and 1968. These are excellent years to compare since the aggregate unemployment rate in these years was quite similar. This is important, for the level of unemployment does affect income shares. Notice, for example, the impact of the higher unemployment rate of 1970 on the share of income received by the lowest quintile. It fell from 5.7 percent in 1968 to 5.5 percent in 1970. Such a decrease in the share of income going to this quintile as unemployment rates rise is not unexpected, for increased general unemployment is most seriously felt by the marginal labor force groups, who are generally low income.

A comparison of the 1947 and 1968 income shares is most revealing. In 1947, the share of the lowest quintile was 5.0 percent compared to 5.7 percent in 1968. This may not seem to be much of a shift but it amounts to an increase of *14* percent in the income share of this group.

Table 3

PERCENTAGE INCOME SHARES FOR FAMILIES,
VARIOUS YEARS, 1947-1970

Income Group	1947	1950	1960	1965	1968	1970
Lowest Quintile	5.0	4.5	4.9	5.3	5.7	5.5
Second Quintile	11.8	12.0	12.0	12.1	12.4	12.0
Third Quintile	17.0	17.4	17.6	17.7	17.7	17.4
Fourth Quintile	23.1	23.5	23.6	23.7	23.7	23.5
Highest Quintile	43.0	42.6	42.0	41.3	40.6	41.6
Highest 5 Percent	17.2	17.0	16.8	15.8	14.0	14.4

Source: U.S. Bureau of the Census, Current Population Survey.

Similar upward shifts can be observed in the second, third, and fourth quintiles, although they represent smaller relative increases in the income shares. At the top of the income distribution, the share of income claimed by the top 20 percent decreased from 43.0 to 40.6 percent, a decline of more than five percent. Even this, though, is misleading. Consider only the top five percent of the income distribution. Their share fell from 17.2 percent to 14.0 percent of all income. This is a decline of almost 20 percent in their share of income. A part of this decline was redistributed to the remaining 15 percent of the top quintile whose income share rose from 25.8 percent to 26.6 percent.

The data of Table 3 suggest a general redistribution of income away from the top of the income distribution to all other groups. This is confirmed when the data for 1947 and 1968 are displayed graphically through the device of Lorenz curves. This is done in Figure 1. The Lorenz curves shown there indicate a clear shift towards greater equality in the income distribution between 1947 and 1968. The amount of the shift can be gauged from the change in the Gini coefficient that occurs in this period. In 1947, it is approximately .363, while in 1968, it is about .332. This represents a decline in the degree of inequality of income distribution of between eight and nine percent. One other point is worth noting. In general, the movement towards greater equality in the personal income distribution is one of a consistent trend and not a sudden sharp thing. This indicates that our basic conclusion about declining income inequality is not an accident that might be attributed to our selection of years for comparison.

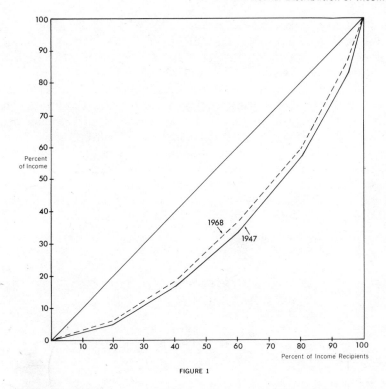

FIGURE 1

II. THE PRESENT PATTERN OF INCOME DISTRIBUTION

The broad conclusion suggested to this point is that, historically, there has been a consistent tendency towards greater equality in the distribution of income in the United States. For those who are interested in social reform, *per se*, this should be an encouraging and enlightening result. However, it by no means puts to rest the question of whether the United States has a "desirable" distribution of income. That is essentially a matter of normative judgment and there is sizable room for disagreement. What is optimal in this respect for one person may be far less than optimal for another. To some, the present income distribution in the United States may still be too unequal, while for others, the movement towards greater equality may have gone too far already. We do not pretend here to offer guidelines for the making of this type judgment. On the other hand, we can provide some perspective on the nature of the existing pattern of income distribution by examining readily available data from the Current Population Survey of the Bureau of the Census.

We have already alluded to certain of these data in Chapter Two. There, we pointed out that the distribution of wage and salary income is more unequal than the distribution of family personal income. Similar data are available describing the distribution of other types of income. These are shown for males in Table 4. Let us first look at the distribution of income derived from dividends, rents, interest, royalties, and estates. The beauty of this set of data is that it describes income strictly from property sources. Clearly, the distribution of this type of income is much more unequal than that of other forms of income. However, two very interesting findings emerge from examining these data. First, of the approximately 70 million men who received income in 1970, over 30 percent had income from property sources. Second, only 0.3 percent of those who receive property income and only 0.1 percent of all recipients of income obtain as much as $25,000 a year from property income. Thus, only a very few individuals (one in a thousand) have property income sufficient in and of itself to place them in the $25,000 and over income category. Further, at the most, only 0.2

Table 4

DISTRIBUTION OF INCOME, BY TYPE,
MALE INCOME RECIPIENTS, 1970

Amount of Income	Dividends, Interest, Rental Income, etc.	Self-Employment		Social Security & RR Retirement	Public Assistance and Welfare	Unemployment and Workmen's Compensation	Private Pensions & Annuities, etc.
		Non-Farm	Farm				
Under $500	70.6 %	20.0 %	38.0 %	5.6 %	32.7 %	36.3 %	24.5 %
$ 500-999	11.1	6.2	9.1	18.3	29.7	22.5	20.6
1000-1499	5.5	4.4	7.4	21.6	17.7	13.9	14.0
1500-1999	3.3	3.5	5.8	28.8	9.1	7.2	12.0
2000-2499	2.2	3.7	5.1	13.6	3.2	5.1	8.0
2500-2999	1.2	2.3	2.8	7.0	2.6	3.3	4.4
3000-3999	1.8	6.3	6.9	4.2	2.5	4.0	7.6
4000-4999	1.1	4.9	4.6	0.8	2.0	2.4	2.8
5000-5999	0.8	5.8	4.0	0.1	0.4	2.1	2.0
6000-6999	0.4	5.2	3.1	0.1	0.1	1.2	1.3
7000-7999	0.3	5.6	2.8	-	-	0.4	0.8
8000-9999	0.3	7.4	3.4	-	0.1	0.9	0.6
10000-14999	0.7	10.7	4.4	-	-	0.7	0.9
15000-24999	0.3	8.3	2.0	-	-	-	0.5
25000 and over	0.3	5.7	0.6	-	-	-	0.2
Number with Income ('000's)	22,322	5,748	2,825	8,759	1,507	7,897	3,311
Median Income	$ 554	$ 4,727	$ 1,199	$ 1,579	$ 790	$ 803	$1,175
Mean Income	$ 848	$ 7,154	$ 2,644	$ 1,606	$ 1,017	$1,374	$ 1,816

Source: U.S. Bureau of the Census, Current Population Survey.

percent of income recipients have sufficient income from property sources to guarantee that their family will be in the top quintile of the personal income distribution.¹¹

Similar estimates from the wage and salary income distribution indicate that 1.2 percent of male income receivers have wage and salary income sufficient to place their family in the $25,000 and over category. Therefore, compared to property income, 12 times as many people have wage and salary income that insures their having $25,000 or more of income. Also, over five percent of male income recipients have wage and salary income that guarantees their family being in the top quintile of the family income distribution. This is over 25 times as many people as would be in that category strictly because of the receipt of property income.

These data suggest again the importance of inequality in the distribution of wage and salary income as a determinant of overall income inequality. They also strike a sharp blow at any stereotype notion of the "idle rich." To see this more clearly, examine the data of Table 5. They show the sources of income for males with income of

Table 5

TYPE OF INCOME 1970, ALL MALES AND ALL MALES WITH INCOME GREATER THAN $25,000

Type of Income	Percent with type of Income	
	All Males	Males with Greater than $25,000
Wage and Salary	80.2	72.4
Wage and Salary Only	43.4	13.1
Self Employment	12.7	37.4
Self Employment Only	4.0	6.1
Other Income	39.1	76.0
Other Income Only	11.5	2.5
Wage and Salary and/or Self-Employment	88.5	97.5

Source: U.S. Bureau of the Census, Current Population Survey.

$25,000 or more in 1970. The most interesting aspect of these data is the proportion of those at this income level who have wage and salary or self-employment income, 97.5 percent. This means that only 2.5 percent of those with very high incomes do not have work related income. Of course, at this income level, non-work related income means primarily property income. By contrast, 11.5 percent of all income recipients have only income from other than work related sources.

Thus, the very wealthy are more closely associated with work activity than the society in general. Part of the explanation for this phenomenon is the reliance of lower income groups on such sources of non-work income as pensions and annuities (both private and public) and government transfer payments. For example, observe in Table 4 the large percentage of those receiving such payments who receive amounts that are less than $2,000 per year. Frequently, these payments are the primary source of income among low income people. This is confirmed by the data of Table 6 which show by income class the proportion of male income recipients who received only non-work related income during 1970. Clearly, the strongest evidence of non-attachment to work related income is found among the low income classes.

Table 6

PERCENT MALES WITHOUT EARNINGS INCOME, BY INCOME CLASS, 1970

Income Class	Percent without Earnings
Under $500	11.1
$ 500—999	21.5
1000—1499	38.2
1500—1999	44.0
2000—2499	34.5
2500—2999	33.2
3000—3999	22.8
4000—4999	14.8
5000—5999	8.0
6000—6999	4.8
7000—7999	2.7
8000—9999	1.7
10000—14999	1.3
15000—24999	1.2
25000 and over	2.5

Source: U.S. Bureau of the Census, Current Population Survey.

Of course, it can be argued that the important consideration is not the numbers who receive particular types of income among the high income groups, but the proportion of their total income that is accounted for by the various income catagories. Table 7 shows these proportions for families with 1970 income less than $25,000 and families with 1970 income of $25,000 or more. Interestingly, the proportion of income accounted for by earnings activity is almost exactly the same, 88.3 percent for those with incomes of $25,000 or more and 88.7 percent for those with incomes less than $25,000. Also, pure property income (dividends, interest, etc.) accounts for only 8.8 percent of family income where income is $25,000 or greater.

While the higher income classes are very substantially dependent on work related income for their economic position in our society, the sources of that income are significantly different from those of the population as a whole. Self-employment income plays a much more important role among the high income group: The proportion of those with incomes of $25,000 or more with this type income is about three times as large as it is for all persons. Similarly, the proportion of total income accounted for by self-employment is about three times greater in the $25,000 and over category than it is in the under $25,000 range. At the same time, the proportion of the $25,000 or greater class with wage and salary income is somewhat less than it is overall (72.4 percent

Table 7

PROPORTION OF INCOME ACCOUNTED FOR BY VARIOUS TYPES OF INCOME, BY INCOME CLASS, FAMILIES, UNITED STATES, 1970

Type of Income	Family Income Level	
	$25,000 or more	Less than $25,000
Wage and salary	68.2%	82.1%
Self-Employment		
Non-farm	18.6	5.3
Farm	1.5	1.3
Dividends, Rent, Interest, etc.	8.8	2.8
Other*	2.9	8.5

Source: U.S. Bureau of the Census, Current Population Survey.

*Other income consists of Social Security benefits, unemployment compensation, workmen's compensation, government employee pensions, railroad retirement benefits, private pensions, annuities, alimony, etc.

versus 80.2 percent) and the proportion of income resulting from wages and salaries is correspondingly less (again, see Table 7). The greater involvement in self-employment activity undoubtedly reflects greater ownership of assets of some form. Possession of such assets permits self-employment activity while non-possession of them limits it. This probably also accounts for the degree of inequality in the distribution of self-employment income. From the Lorenz curves of Figure 2, it can be seen that self-employment income is even more unequally distributed than wage and salary income. Thus, we find that both components of work related income are more unequally distributed than family personal income.

III. CONCLUSIONS

What can we say in summary? Several aspects of the distribution of income in the United States have been discussed and a number of.

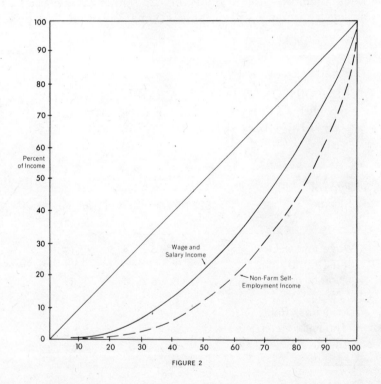

FIGURE 2

important broad conclusions have been advanced. Among them are: (1) The long run tendency in the United States has been in the direction of greater equality of income distribution, (2) this trend has continued in the post World War II period, and (3) those in the upper reaches of the income distribution are extremely dependent on work related activity as a source of income. This set of conclusions has important implications. Primarily, it would seem to indicate, rather clearly, that the simplistic version of the backwash thesis, i.e., the one that employs an absolute definition of poverty, has little validity. There is simply no way in which it can be reconciled with the evidence of decreasing income inequality. Alternative definitions of poverty may yield somewhat different conclusions, though. This will be explored in more .depth in the next chapter.

Second, the general findings of Chapter Two are confirmed, namely, that the notion that those at the upper tail of the income distribution derive their advantageous position primarily from non-work related sources of income is fallacious. Only a very small fraction of those with high incomes do not engage in work type activity. This would seem to refute the cliche-like concept of the "idle rich," at least as it might be applied to the top five percent of the income distribution.

Collectively, these findings indicate that the United States has been progressing persistently in the direction of a more egalitarian society, one in which the relative economic differentials among people are being narrowed with the passage of time. They also suggest that the key to economic success in the United States is the capacity to command work related income in the labor markets of our society. Since this capacity would seem to depend on the possession of differential amounts of human capital, the obvious implication is that economic rewards in the United States are, to a very substantial extent, a function of the personal abilities of people, although there are certainly exceptions to this rule. Again, this is suggestive of a society that might be characterized as a "meritocracy," a society in which the major sources of differences in economic rewards are variations in individual abilities and merit. This is an intriguing hypothesis,one that is, we might add, in substantial conflict with much of the existing poverty literature which seems to argue that poverty has its roots in a lack of opportunity for merit and ability to command economic rewards. Consequently, we will examine these competing hypotheses extensively in the chapters that follow.

FOOTNOTES

[1]Academicians are a particularly pertinent example, for they ought to be better informed, more objective, and certainly more deliberate in their judgment than the average citizen. Unfortunately, where matters of the pocketbook are concerned, many of them are virtually indistinguishable in their thought processes from the typical member of society as a whole.

[2]For evidence along these lines, see "Coping With Adversity: Report on the Economic Status of the Profession, 1971-1972," *Bulletin, American Association of University Professors*, Summer Issue, June 1972, pp. 178-243. Table 7 of that article (p. 186) shows that the

median nine-month average compensation for full professors for the academic year 1971-72 was $20,850. For associate professors, the median was $15,790; assistant professors, $12,980; and instructors, $10,430. Further, those data indicate that about 90 percent of full professors and 30 percent of associate professors receive compensation sufficient to place them in the top quintile of the society's family income distribution. Since this only covers nine month compensation, actual family incomes would be somewhat higher due to extra compensation for additional teaching assignments, royalties, honoraria, and working wives.

[3]It is difficult to estimate what income level will support a "wealthy" standard of living. However, keep in mind that only one family in 200 has an income in excess of $50,000 and I suspect that the consensus notion of "wealthy" would require at least this much income.

[4]$16,243 to be exact.

[5]Lee Soltow, "Economic Inequality in the United States in the Period from 1790 to 1860," *Journal of Economic History*, December 1971, pp. 822-839.

[6]Guillaume Thomas-Francois Raynal, *A Philisophical and Political History of the Settlements and Trade of the Europeans in the East and West Indies*, trans. J. Justamond, 4 vols. Edinburgh, 1776, IV, p. 310.

[7]Soltow, *Ibid.*

[8]Lee Soltow, "Evidence on Income Inequality in the United States, 1866-1965," *Journal of Economic History*, June 1969, pp. 279-286.

[9]Simon Kuznets, *Shares of Upper Income Groups in Income and Savings.* New York: National Bureau of Economic Research, 1953.

[10]"The American Distribution of Income: A Structural Problem," *op. cit.*

[11]This estimate is derived by multiplying 0.3 by the proportion of male income recipients who received income of the dividends, rental, interest, etc. type.

POVERTY AND ECONOMIC GROWTH

One of the great debates of the past decade has been whether economic growth is an effective device for eliminating poverty. In fact, this argument was central to a good bit of the initial formulation of the poverty problem. Witness the 1964 statement by the Council of Economic Advisors:[1]

> ...open exits [from poverty] mean little to those who cannot move — to the millions who are caught in the web of poverty through illiteracy, lack of skills, racial discrimination, broken homes, and ill health—*conditions which are hardly touched by prosperity and growth.* (emphasis supplied)

This is simply the backwash thesis, which holds that the economic status of meaningful numbers of people is relatively unaffected by the process of economic growth. To a certain extent, we have already been exploring this hypothesis. As noted in the previous chapter, when an absolute level of real income definition of poverty is employed, the available evidence lends no support at all to the backwash thesis. To recapitulate, for the backwash phenomenon to be operative in these circumstances, economic growth must be accompanied by increases in the degree of inequality found in the income distribution due to the necessary "stretching out" of the distribution that is implied by the backwash concept. Given the clear evidence of reductions in income inequality of the post-World War II period, this version of the backwash hypothesis must be rejected.

I. NEUTRALITY OF ECONOMIC GROWTH AND THE "BACKWASH" THESIS

A more subtle variant of the proposition exists, however. Assume a relativistic definition of poverty such as that suggested by Fuchs. Clearly, this has the effect of introducing a substantial degree of stability into the poverty rate. In fact, as we pointed out earlier, the range of variation in the poverty rate, as calculated using the Fuchs criterion, is about two percentage points in the post-World War II period. Such a situation is quite suggestive of the basic notion implied in the backwash thesis.

If the backwash hypothesis is interpreted in this fashion, all that is required for it to be valid is that the impact of economic growth on the income distribution be "neutral." To illustrate what is meant by economic growth being neutral with respect to the income distribution, consider Figure 1. In that diagram, two income distributions are shown, an initial one (denoted by a dotted line) and one that has been shifted positively (indicated by a solid line) by a general increase in the level of real economic activity, i.e., by economic growth. Now, arbitrarily select an income level B that is substantially less than the median. If the impact of economic growth is perfectly neutral with respect to the income distribution, all incomes included in the

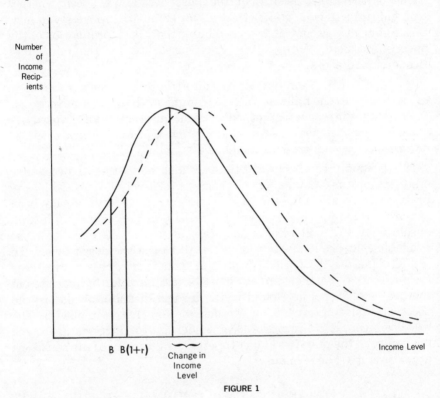

FIGURE 1

distribution will be increased by exactly the same percentage. Thus, a ten percent increase in income levels would produce a ten percent increase in every income level. Of course, perfect neutrality of this type would never exist. Certainly, some individual incomes might not increase by as much as ten percent and others might increase by more than ten percent. For our purposes, though, we are interested in how economic growth affects different income classes, not specific individuals. Thus, if the impact of growth is neutral, we would expect the proportion of individuals in the initial income distribution with incomes less than B to be the same as the proportion in the second distribution with incomes less than B(1+r) where r is the general rate of growth in income. If the proportion in the second case with incomes less than B(1+r) is greater than expected, growth may be considered to be biased *against* the low income portion of the income distribution while biased growth in *favor* of the relatively poor would be indicated by the proportion with incomes less than B(1+r) being less than expected.

Alternatively, neutrality of growth is evidenced by the proportion of income recipients in the second distribution with incomes less than B being exactly the same as the proportion in the initial distribution with incomes less than B(1+r). In this context, growth biased against the poor would be indicated by the proportion in the second distribution with incomes less than B being greater than expected and vice-versa. Either of these views of the neutrality notion can be employed to structure an empirical test of whether growth is neutral, biased against, or biased in favor of the poor in the United States. On the basis of what has already been said, we would expect to find that growth, at the least, is neutral with respect to the income distribution with a very substantial probability that it will be biased in *favor* of the poor. This follows from the earlier evidence of a tendency toward greater income equality in the United States. A decrease in inequality implies that incomes at the lower end of the income distribution increase relative to those at the upper end of the distribution. In an economy marked by increases in real income, this should be reflected as growth that is biased in favor of the poor.

For the purposes of empirically evaluating the neutrality concept, the necessary calculations have been made using the second approach to viewing neutrality. The results are shown in Table I for six different income boundaries: $2,000, $3,000, $4,000, $5,000, $15,000, and $25,000. Four of these are low income levels and two are high income. The low income ones are chosen for obvious reasons and the two high income boundaries are included to obtain some insight into whether growth is neutral or biased with respect to the high income portion of the income distribution. The latter is important, for we are also interested in the extent to which those at the upper tail of the income distribution profit from economic growth. It is often maintained that while growth may assist those at the bottom of the income distribution it benefits those at the upper end even more.[2]

The Table I estimates of the proportion of families with income levels less than the chosen boundary are calculated assuming neutral growth over the interval in question. These may then be compared with the actual proportion. If these are the same, growth is neutral. If the actual proportion is less than the neutral growth proportion, growth is biased in favor of those with incomes below the income boundary in question. Seven time intervals are examined for each income level. In the case of the low income boundaries, the preponderance (19 of 28 instances) of

Table 1

ACTUAL AND NEUTRAL GROWTH PROPORTION
OF FAMILIES WITH ANNUAL INCOMES BELOW
SELECTED INCOME BOUNDARIES,
UNITED STATES, 1959-1969

Time Interval and Income Boundary	Neutral Growth Proportion at end of Interval	Actual Proportion	Deviation (Actual— Neutral)
$2,000			
1959-1963	11.2 %	10.6 %	-0.6 %
1963-1964	9.9	9.5	-0.4
1964-1965	8.8	8.9	0.1
1965-1966	8.1	7.7	-0.4
1966-1967	6.8	6.4	-0.4
1967-1968	5.6	5.1	-0.5
1968-1969	4.5	4.6	0.1
$3,000			
1959-1963	19.0	18.5	-0.5
1963-1964	17.4	17.6	0.2
1964-1965	16.2	16.1	-0.1
1965-1966	13.9	14.3	0.4
1966-1967	12.8	12.3	-0.5
1967-1968	11.1	10.2	-0.9
1968-1969	8.9	9.2	0.3
$4,000			
1959-1963	27.3	27.2	-0.1
1963-1964	24.9	26.0	1.1
1964-1965	24.1	23.8	-0.3
1965-1966	21.8	21.1	-0.7
1966-1967	19.1	18.6	-0.5
1967-1968	16.8	16.2	-0.6
1968-1969	14.2	14.5	0.3
$5,000			
1959-1963	36.6	36.2	-0.4
1963-1964	34.0	34.6	0.6
1964-1965	32.2	31.7	-0.5
1965-1966	29.2	28.2	-1.0
1966-1967	25.6	25.1	-0.5
1967-1968	22.6	22.2	-0.4
1968-1969	19.6	19.9	0.3
$15,000			
1959-1963	94.4	94.5	0.1
1963-1964	93.7	93.8	0.1
1964-1965	92.5	92.4	-0.1
1965-1966	90.7	90.8	0.1
1966-1967	88.8	87.8	-1.0
1967-1968	84.6	85.2	0.6
1968-1969	80.0	80.8	0.8
$25,000			
1959-1963	98.9	98.9	0.0
1963-1964	98.7	99.0	0.3
1964-1965	98.6	98.6	0.0
1965-1966	98.3	98.3	0.0
1966-1967	97.8	97.5	-0.3
1967-1968	96.9	97.4	0.5
1968-1969	96.5	96.3	-0.2

Source: *Current Population Reports, P-60 Series.*

differences between the actual and neutral growth proportions is in a direction that indicates biased growth in favor of the low income groups. Also, the arithmetic mean of the deviations is clearly negative in all four cases, which indicates that the effect of growth is biased in favor of these groups.

At the upper end of the income distribution, half of the deviations are either 0.0 or 0.1 percentage points. Of the remainder, three are negative and four are positive. This would seem to suggest that growth is probably neutral with respect to the upper tail of the income distribution. These results are perfectly consistent with the previous evidence of decreasing inequality in the income distribution. If economic growth has effects that are neutral with respect to the high income groups and biased in favor of the low income classes, the net result should be a systematic redistribution of income in favor of the lower income groups.

II. INCOME REDISTRIBUTION AND THE FUCHS' DEFINITION OF POVERTY

The evidence with respect to the neutrality phenomenon indicates that even in the presence of a relative definition of poverty, there are indications that economic growth has the potential to produce some reduction in the poverty rate. How much, though, remains a question, a question that again takes us back to the fundamental problem of what constitutes an optimal distribution of income. If we knew what the optimal distribution of income was, we would automatically define the optimal level of poverty. For many people, that optimum would be zero. If we assume a definition of poverty such as Fuchs's, this would amount to truncating the income distribution at the lower end at one-half the median income. It is highly unlikely that economic growth by itself will be able to accomplish such an objective. Quite frankly, a substantial amount of deliberate income redistribution through the device of transfer payment income would probably be required to reduce poverty, as defined by Fuchs, to zero.

The necessary amount of redistribution can be roughly estimated by assigning those families with income less than Fuchs's poverty line an income equal to one-half the median income. As an example, in Table 2 we have recalculated the 1970 shares of income under two sets of assumptions. The first assumes that the redistribution required to upgrade the incomes of those below the poverty line is entirely at the expense of the top five percent of the income distribution and the second allocates the redistribution proportionately across the remainder of the income distribution.[3] From these distributions, Gini coefficients have been estimated and they indicate that approximately a 15 to 20 percent reduction in inequality would be required to achieve zero poverty. While this is an interesting conclusion, it still does not

Table 2

ESTIMATED INCOME SHARES, 1970, BY QUINTILE
AND TOP 5 PERCENT OF INCOME DISTRIBUTION,
ASSUMING FUCH'S POVERTY DEFINITION

	Income Share		
Quintile	Actual	Assuming Proportional Redistribution	Assuming All Redistribution from Top 5 Percent
Lowest	5.5 %	9.3 %	9.3 %
Second	12.0	11.5	12.0
Third	17.4	16.7	17.4
Fourth	23.5	22.6	23.5
Highest	41.6	39.9	37.8
Top 5%	14.4	13.8	10.6

Source: *Current Population Reports, P-60 Series.*

answer the basic question of what is the optimal distribution of income for the society. That is an extremely intractable problem. However, what we have said till now does imply that economic growth will not be especially effective in reducing poverty if poverty is defined in relativistic terms. This is particularly true, given the nature of the shifts in income distributions that have been taking place in the post-World War II United States.

The evidence shows a clear redistribution of income, but the pattern of redistribution has not been from the very rich to the very poor. Instead, it has been from the very rich to the remainder of the society. Consequently, the economic position of the very poor has improved dramatically relative to the very rich, but has remained almost unchanged relative to those in the middle of the income distribution. For example, in 1947, the share of income of the bottom quintile of the income distribution was 29 percent as large as the share of both the middle quintile and the top five percent of income recipients. By 1968, the lowest quintile's share was equal to 41 percent of the share of the top five percent but only 32 percent of the share of the middle quintile. Clearly, relative to the quintile that spans the median income point, the very poor had improved their position only imperceptibly despite substantial income redistribution. Thus, if economic growth would continue to be biased with respect to the income distribution in a fashion similar to that already observed, poverty in the Fuchs sense would not be substantially affected.

III. INCOME REDISTRIBUTION AND THE ABSOLUTE GAP DEFINITION OF POVERTY

A third possible method of defining poverty — the absolute gap approach — was mentioned in Chapter One. It has been given serious consideration in the previously cited Thurow-Lucas study that was prepared for the Joint Economic Committee of the Congress.[4] In that study, much has been made of the fact that the gap between the average incomes of the top and bottom quintiles of the income distribution has been widening. Specifically, it has been pointed out that between 1947 and 1970, that gap increased from less than $11,000 to more than $19,000 in constant 1969 dollars. The authors of the study suggest that this widening gap presents a serious problem for American society. In fact, the study has been advertised as indicating that the "rich" are getting "richer" and the "poor" are getting "poorer." Implicitly, this amounts to defining poverty in terms of the absolute gap approach, since it suggests that there is something desirable in maintaining a stable absolute difference in incomes between the high income and low income groups.

The method of defining poverty as existing whenever income falls below the median by some fixed number of dollars (in real terms) is novel, but it yields some curious conclusions when pursued fully. For example, consider the basic impact on the poverty rate of what we have previously defined as neutral economic growth. If substantial growth of this type occurred, its effect would be to actually *increase* the poverty rate. All that neutral economic growth does is to increase all income levels by the same percentage. This can only have the effect of widening the gap between the low and high income groups. In fact, with neutral economic growth, the logical implication is that *the greater the growth rate in the economy, the greater will be the poverty rate.* This is certainly a strange conclusion. Actually, with anything but economic growth that is unbelievably biased in favor of the low income groups, growth can only serve to increase the poverty rate when poverty is defined in this fashion.

To pursue this point somewhat further, consider what would eventually happen to the poverty rate if sustained neutral economic growth were the order of the day. Under such conditions, an absolute gap poverty rate would asymptotically approach 50 percent. The only way in which this could be avoided would be through massive redistribution of income through tax and subsidy policies. To illustrate how much redistribution is potentially involved, let us re-estimate income shares for the top and bottom quintiles of the 1970 income distribution, assuming that the absolute difference (in real terms) between the mean incomes of these two groups was the same as it was in 1947. Given this assumption, the lowest quintile's share of total income in 1970 would be 13.5 percent, while that for the top quintile would be 33.7 percent. These are tremendous shifts in the distribution of income.

Perhaps the clearest evidence of the impact of the absolute gap poverty definition is provided by the data of Table 3. In that table, the 1947 poverty rate has been calculated on the basis of the Fuchs suggestion of one-half the median income as a poverty criterion. With this established, the absolute gap (in real dollars) between the median level of income and the poverty boundary is held constant through 1970. The result is an increase in the poverty rate from 19.7 percent to 32.7 percent. And, if economic growth had been greater, the increases in the poverty rate would have been even more substantial.

What a potpourri of findings! Obviously, the relationship between the poverty rate and economic growth depends on how poverty is defined. Growth is an effective factor in eliminating poverty if poverty

Table 3

POVERTY RATES CALCULATED ON BASIS OF ABSOLUTE GAP POVERTY DEFINITION ASSUMING 1947 POVERTY LINE BASED ON FUCH'S DEFINITION , 1947-1970

Year	Estimated Poverty Rate	Poverty Line (1970 $)
1947	19.7%	$2,629
1950	20.6	2,755
1958	25.9	4,196
1959	27.6	4,586
1960	27.9	4,746
1961	28.2	4,827
1962	28.2	5,029
1963	29.2	5,297
1964	30.1	5,597
1965	30.5	5,929
1966	30.6	6,347
1967	31.0	6,655
1968	31.3	7,003
1969	32.2	7,360
1970	32.7	7,237

Source: *Current Population Reports, P-60 Series.*

is defined in absolute terms. However, it has much less impact if poverty is measured by a relative standard and actually increases the absolute gap type poverty rate. Thus, one can have almost any view he chooses about the importance of economic growth in eliminating poverty depending on what he means by poverty. But, very clearly, if definitions of the type employed by the Federal Government are used, growth is an important factor in reducing poverty.

IV. THE ELASTICITY OF POVERTY WITH RESPECT TO ECONOMIC GROWTH

In the remainder of this chapter, we will focus on some additional aspects of the behavior of the poverty rate in the United States. To facilitate this discussion, we will define poverty in absolute terms at $3,000 of family income in 1963 prices. Using such a definition, we can examine in detail the relationship between poverty and the general progress of the economy in the post-World War II period in America. To begin, the linkage between the poverty rate and the median level of family income is shown graphically in Figure 2. Median family income is being used here as an index of general economic growth in the society. Obviously, the relationship between these two variables is extremely strong. More precisely, over the period 1947-1968, the

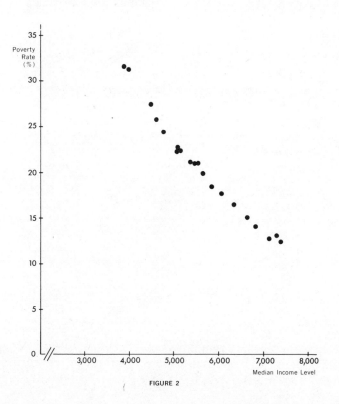

FIGURE 2

elasticity of poverty with respect to median family income is about -1.4, i.e., a one percent increase in median family income produced a 1.4 percent decrease in poverty.[5] In addition, the poverty rate is also sensitive to variations in the aggregate unemployment rate, although to a much lesser extent. A one percent increase in the unemployment rate will produce a 0.1 percent increase in the poverty rate. Interestingly, there is evidence that these relationships were undergoing change over the period. Through 1964, the elasticity of the poverty rate with respect to median family income was significantly lower at about -1.3 and the elasticity with respect to unemployment was about half that reported for the entire period 1947-1968.[6] The impact of these changes is shown by Table 4, which contains estimates of the poverty rate for years following 1964 based on the 1947-1964 relationship between poverty and the two measures of aggregate economic activity that have been mentioned. When these estimates are compared with the actual poverty rates, it is very obvious that the 1947-1964 relationship overpredicts the poverty rate for ensuing years by amounts that are reasonably significant. This suggests the presence of some type of structural change in the relationship between the level of poverty and aggregate economic conditions.

The quantitative importance of this structural change can be measured by conventional statistical means.[7] Such an analysis reveals

Table 4

PREDICTED AND ACTUAL POVERTY RATES, UNITED STATES, 1965 THROUGH 1970

Year	Poverty Rate (%)	
	Actual	Predicted
1965	16.8%	16.4%
1966	15.2	15.3
1967	14.2	15.1
1968	12.8	13.9
1969	12.5	13.2
1970	13.1	13.8

that in the post-1964 period, the poverty rate fell about nine percent more each year than it should have, given the changes in median family income and aggregate unemployment that took place.[8] Even more interesting than the structural change itself is the reason for it. Accounting for the shift involves some speculation on our part, but certain explanations can be rather effectively eliminated. First, there is the possibility that the decrease in the degree of inequality in the overall income distribution will explain the change. A brief review of the evidence with respect to that change suggests that there was an acceleration in the decrease in inequality after 1964. Between 1947 and 1965, the relative share of the top five percent of the income distribution declined from 17.2 to 15.8 percent and the share of the bottom quintile rose from 5.0 to 5.3 percent. On the other hand, the changes in these shares between 1965 and 1968 (a three year period compared to the 18 years between 1947 and 1965) were even greater. For example, the share of the top five percent fell another 1.8 percentage points and that for the bottom quintile rose 0.4 percentage points. Clearly, inequality declined much more rapidly each year after 1965 than it did before.

While the acceleration in the decline in income inequality cannot be denied, its impact on the elasticity of poverty with respect to median family income was probably minimal. The reason for this is that all income groups other than the top five percent were the beneficiaries of income redistribution. Consequently, the share of the bottom quintile changed very little relative to the share of the middle quintile which contains the median income level. All though the post-World War II period, the share of the bottom quintile is about 30 percent of the share of the middle quintile. Thus, income redistribution has probably contributed very little to the change in the relationship between the poverty rate and median family income.

A second possible explanation for the shift in the structural relationship between the poverty rate and the level of median family income is that the civil rights revolution has been successful in reducing the impact of economic discrimination against non-whites and that this has produced a more rapid decrease in poverty than expected. Plausible? Surely! However, it is not supported by the evidence. For this explanation to be valid, the percentage decline in poverty after 1964 among non-whites relative to that among whites should be greater than it was in the period 1947-1964. Table 5 presents data on this point and they indicate rather clearly that, if anything, the reverse is true. The relationship between the rate of change in poverty by race does not shift in the appropriate direction to support the hypothesis that a decline in discrimination has produced an increase in the responsiveness of the poverty rate to changes in the general level of economic activity.

But, what else might account for the change we have observed in the poverty rate-median family income relationship? Could it be that the onset of substantial anti-poverty programs at the federal level has had some significant impact in reducing the poverty rate beyond what would be expected simply as the result of economic growth? Possibly.

Again, though, the evidence is not persuasive. Given the tremendous thrust in recent years in the direction of improving the relative economic status of non-whites, it is reasonable to believe that the impact of the various federal programs designed to reduce poverty would be felt disproportionately among non-whites. However, as already noted, there is no reason to suppose that this has been the case. Admittedly, this is indirect evidence and it does not rule out the possibility that the impact of these programs will explain the unexpected decline in the poverty rate. It does make one suspicious, though.

Table 5

PERCENT DECREASES IN FAMILY POVERTY RATES, BY RACE, 1947-1964 AND 1964-1970

Period	Percent Decrease in Poverty Rate	
	White Families	Negro Families
1947-1964	44.4%	42.8%
1964-1970	31.0	26.5

Source: *Current Population Reports, P-60 Series.*

This still leaves us without an answer to our problem. The inability to find a reasonable one may simply be the result of our looking in the wrong place. We have been searching for some factor unique to the post-1964 period that will account for the observed shift, whereas we perhaps should be seeking an explanation that turns on something peculiar to the 1947-1964 period that operated to make the observed elasticity of poverty with respect to median family income less than it normally is. A real possibility of this being the case exists. The immediate post-World War II period was marked by the maturing of the Old Age Survivors Disability and Health Insurance (OASDHI) system in the United States. The major impact of this was on the relative income levels of families with an aged head. As retirement benefits became more readily available, there was a tendency for the labor force participation rate among the aged to fall.[9] The result was a decline in the relative income position of aged families. In 1947, median family income of aged families was about 60 percent of that for all families. By the mid-1960's, this had declined to about 50 percent, at which point it stabilized.

A few simple statistics will illustrate what happened after 1947. As of 1947, about ten percent of aged males were receiving old age benefits under the Social Security system, while by the mid- to late 1960's, upwards of 85 percent were recipients of this type of income. Also, in 1947 the labor force participation rate among aged males was 47.8 percent and by the late 1960's, it had declined to about 27 percent. Apparently, there was a substitution of non-work for work related income on the part of the aged. A more detailed analysis of this will be presented later. For now, we will simply observe its occurrence. However, by the mid-1960's, the impact of this substitution on the economy had largely run its course. In effect, the interval from 1947 to the mid-1960's can be characterized as one in which the American economy was undergoing a substantial structural change as it adapted to the presence of a full blown Social Security system.[10] Due to the reduction in the relative income of the aged that accompanied this adjustment, the elasticity of poverty with respect to median family income was reduced below its normal level.[11] But, as the adaptation to the presence of the Social Security system was largely completed (in the mid-1960's), this retarding influence on the elimination of poverty was no longer operative. The result is an increase in the observed sensitivity of the poverty rate to increases in overall median family income.

What is the significance of this explanation of the observed shift in the elasticity of poverty with respect to median family income? Simply this: All the projections of future poverty rates based on extrapolations from data taken largely from the 1947 to 1964 period are decidedly suspect. For example, take the famous projections of the Council of Economic Advisers made in 1964. They are shown in Table 6.[12] Two sets of estimates of future poverty rates are provided, one assuming economic growth such as that observed between 1947 and 1956 and the other based on 1956-1963 growth patterns. The latter are the more pessimistic since general levels of growth were lower in the period 1956-1963 than between 1947 and 1956. When compared with the current poverty rates (also shown in Table 6), it is clear that even the optimistic projections have been exceeded, partly because economic growth in the mid- and late 1960's exceeded expectations and partly due to the implicit use of an elasticity of poverty with respect to growth that is biased downwards.[13]

Actually, it appears that the true elasticity of poverty with respect to median family income is probably about - 2.0 rather than - 1.4.[14] On the basis of such an elasticity, it can be estimated that with a three percent growth rate in real median family income (which is roughly equal to the 1947-1956 growth rate), the poverty rate in 1980 would be about 6.5 percent instead of the Council's optimistic estimate of ten percent.[15] Consequently, one is tempted to conclude that the potential for economic growth to eliminate poverty (defined in absolute terms) is sizable. How sizable can be inferred from some simple projections that

Table 6

COUNCIL OF ECONOMIC ADVISERS
1964 PREDICTED POVERTY RATES AND ACTUAL RATE,
UNITED STATES, 1970 AND 1980

| Year | Council Predictions | | Actual Poverty Rate |
	Assuming 1947-56 Growth Rate	Assuming 1957-62 Growth Rate	
1970*	15%	17%	13%
1980	10	13	---

*Council of Economic Advisers' estimates based on interpolation.

can be made by assuming various unemployment rates and growth rates in median family income.

In Figure 3, we have assumed various unemployment rates and levels of median family income and estimated the poverty rates that would be associated with them. Four different unemployment rates have been used (three, four, five, and six percent). From these estimates it appears, for example, that an eight percent poverty rate would be associated with a level of real median family income (1963 prices) of about $9,000 and an unemployment rate between three and four percent. More interesting is how long it would take to achieve such a poverty rate. This can be determined from Figure 4, which depicts graphically the behavior of the poverty rate over time (1970-1990) assuming four percent unemployment and two, three, and four percent growth rates in median family income. Four percent growth corresponds roughly to the rate of the 1960's, three percent to the period 1947-1956, and two percent to the immediate post-1956 period.

From Figure 4, it can be seen that a four percent growth rate will produce an eight percent poverty rate by about 1975, a three percent growth rate would postpone this result till 1977, and a two percent growth rate would delay it still further until about 1980. The implication is clear — differences in growth rates have a substantial effect on the behavior of the poverty rate. Even so, we would prefer to know more about the likely returns from future economic growth. Will they be sufficient to justify relying heavily on growth as a policy approach to eliminating poverty? To answer that question, consider the percentage difference in the poverty rates associated with different growth rates at various points in time. For example, Figure 4 indicates that by 1975 the difference in the poverty rate as the result of a three percent

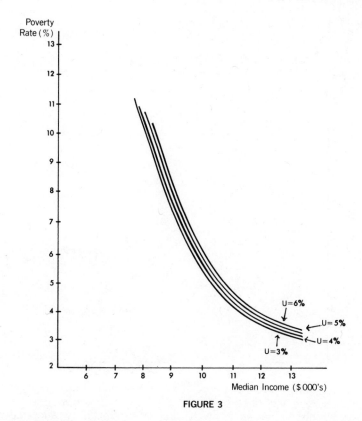

Poverty
Rate (%)

Median Income ($ 000's)

FIGURE 3

growth rate rather than a two percent one is of the order of 13 percent
(1.4 percentage points) and by 1980, the difference is 21 percent (1.7
percentage points). Further, the difference between a two percent and
four percent growth rate is 23 percent in 1975 (2.4 percentage points)
and 35 percent in 1980 (2.9 percentage points). This would seem to
indicate substantial returns (in terms of eliminating poverty) from the
presence of higher growth rates.

At the same time, it should be realized that there are limits to what
growth can do, particularly once poverty is reduced below the ten
percent level. In the late 1960's, the poverty rate was falling about 1.0
percentage points a year. The best we can expect during the 1970's
would probably be the poverty decline associated with a four percent
growth rate, which would be about 0.7 percentage points a year. Three
percent growth would yield an average annual decline of about 0.6
percentage points and two percent growth, an 0.4 to 0.5 yearly percentage point reduction. Of course, the slowing in the yearly reduction
in poverty discussed here may be purely academic since the poverty
definition will probably have been adjusted upward by the end of the
decade. If this does happen, we will merely recycle through another

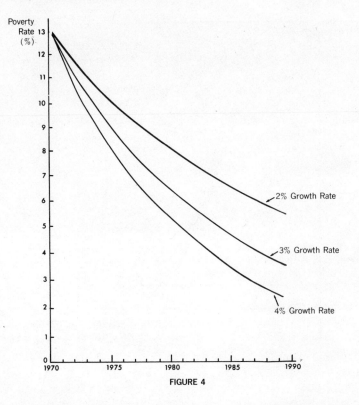

FIGURE 4

period in which economic growth can be remarkably successful in eliminating poverty. Keep in mind that in the 1960's the poverty rate was reduced by about 40 percent. Given the fact that the adjustment to the presence of the Social Security system has been largely accomplished, the returns from growth in the 1970's might be even more spectacular.

V. CONCLUSIONS

Some general conclusions are in order. Broadly speaking, we have argued that economic growth has played and is likely to play a substantial role in eliminating poverty in the United States. Its greatest impact is found, of course, when poverty is defined in absolute terms. The evidence in this case is simply overwhelming that nothing like a backwash phenomenon exists *in general* in the United States. When poverty is viewed in a relativistic manner, the case for growth is not nearly as strong although even here there are indications that growth is not neutral with respect to the distribution of income. Rather, it appears to be biased in favor of the lower tail of the income distribution. This suggests that growth does have some impact on relative poverty, although it appears to be fairly small. Finally, if something like an absolute gap poverty definition is used, growth has nothing to contribute to eliminating poverty. In fact, unless it is accompanied by massive income redistribution, it will merely make matters worse. However, this approach to defining poverty remains so questionable that it does not seem to provide an adequate basis for demeaning the potential contribution of economic growth as a policy approach to eliminating poverty.

FOOTNOTES

[1] United States Congress, *Economic Opportunity Act of 1964*. Hearings before the Subcommittee on the War on Poverty Program of the Committee on Education and Labor, House of Representatives, 88th Congress, 2nd Session, Washington, D.C., pp. 26-30.

[2] This is an integral part of the "backwash" thesis alluded to throughout this volume. See Galbraith, *op. cit.*, and Harrington, *op. cit.*

[3] These shares are estimated by giving the lowest 19 percent of the income distribution an income equal to one-half the median. Knowing this, we can calculate an estimate of the average income of the lowest quintile under these conditions and compare it to the estimated average income from the actual distribution. This comparison yields the factor by which the income share of the lowest quintile must be increased. This procedure tells us that Fuchs' redistribution would require a shift of 3.8 percent of all income to the lowest quintile. This shift is then distributed across all income groups according to the proportion of income received by the top 80 percent that accrues to a particular quintile to arrive at one set of redistribution estimates. The second set takes all the redistributed income from the share of the top five percent of the income distribution.

[4] *Op. cit.*

[5] This estimate is derived by fitting a log linear multiple regression equation of the form:

$$\log P = \log a + b \log Y + c \log U + e$$

where P denotes the poverty rate, Y is median family income, U is the unemployment rate, and e is a random error term.

[6] For details, see my *Manpower Economics*, Richard D. Irwin, Inc., Homewood, Illinois, 1971, Chapter 10.

[7] This is done by including a time drift variable in the multiple regression equation.

[8] This is estimated from the coefficient of the time drift variable in the multiple regression equation.

[9] Two explanations of this phenomenon have been offered. One interprets it as reflecting a substitution of leisure for income by the aged. The

other argues that the lower participation rate is the result of the aged being "pushed" out of the labor force, in part, because employers feel that since OASDHI benefits are available, they are freer to displace older workers. These alternatives will be discussed in Chapter Eight.

[10]This is discussed in detail in my *The Retirement Decision: An Exploratory Essay*, Research Report No. 9, Social Security Administration, Washington, D.C., 1965.

[11]This has a significant impact since the aged are heavily represented among the poor. As many as 20 percent of the poor are aged 65 and over.

[12]Growth in median family income proceeded at 2.93 percent per year between 1947 and 1956 and only 2.18 percent per year between 1957 and 1963.

[13]At that time (the mid-1960's), I argued that the poverty rate would decline more rapidly than predicted by the Council of Economic Advisers. My predictions have been borne out, but not for the right reasons. My conclusions were based on an inappropriate specification of the relationship between median family income and poverty. However, in no way did my analysis at that time take into account the phenomenon of the impact of the adjustment to the OASDHI system on the observed elasticity of poverty with respect to median family income. For details of this matter, see my "The Foundations of the War on Poverty," *American Economic Review*, March 1965, pp. 122-131; Henry Aaron, "The Foundations of the War on Poverty Reexamined," *American Economic Review*, December 1967, pp. 1229-1240; and my "Reply," *Ibid.*, pp. 1241-1243.

[14]This elasticity is based on the observed relationship between the poverty rate and median family income that has prevailed in the past several years.

[15]This predicted poverty rate is almost identical to that provided in my "Foundations of the War On Poverty," *op. cit.* However, for the reasons noted earlier, the two predictions are based on different analyses.

THE HERITAGE OF POVERTY

One of the more frequently encountered arguments in discussions of the causes of poverty is the idea that one's economic status is materially influenced by the economic circumstances of his parents. This gives rise to what has almost become a cliche, the conventional wisdom that poverty is passed from one generation to another in an almost inexorable fashion. As with many bits of conventional wisdom, there is a sizable element of truth in this proposition. There is something like a "cruel legacy of poverty," to borrow a term from a Council of Economic Advisers statement.[1] However, given this (and more information about the extent of this phenomenon will be provided later), there are still many questions to be answered about the precise operation of the mechanism that transmits economic status from generation to generation. And, might I add, the conventional wisdom on this score is frequently something quite a bit less than profound.

If we think in terms of our previous discussion of the sources of differential claims to money income in the United States, two obvious ways in which economic status might be transferred between generations come to mind. First, through the simple transfer of property assets income generating capacity could be rather straightforwardly passed on to children. Second, it is possible that, in some fashion, possession of the attributes that command what we have called human resource income is transferable between generations. From the standpoint of explaining poverty, the latter explanation is most appealing. After all, it is not really the lack of property income that condemns people to poverty. Many people who have income levels that are well beyond the poverty level have little in the way of property income. And, as we have pointed out earlier, even those at the very top of the income distribution are heavily dependent on non-property income. Thus, to the extent that poverty is transmitted from one generation to another, it would appear to be through children acquiring differential access to human resource income.

Let us explore somewhat further exactly what is involved in being able to command human resource income in the labor markets of the American economy. Actually, this translates into having a certain set of skills and aptitudes that the market place has determined to be socially useful. However, exactly what are those skills and aptitudes and how might they be acquired? Certain of them are of a type that one obtains by undergoing training of some kind, such as that dispensed by vocational and professional schools. Others, though, are of a more general variety that do not have their basis in specific training programs. These can be thought of as a broad package of abilities that determine one's capacity to perform tasks that are common to a wide range of economic endeavors. Frequently, a minimum command of these general skills may be a prerequisite for the acquiring of the training that imparts particular skills. For example, a certain level of proficiency of a general kind is necessary before one is considered capable of receiving the special training required of a medical doctor or a nuclear scientist. By now, it should be clear that this broad package of general skills comprises what is normally called "intelligence." At the risk of opening a Pandora's Box of difficulties, it is necessary that we digress somewhat and interject a discussion of the concept of intelligence as it is generally understood. This must be done, if for no other reason than the fact there appears to be a significant relationship between what we consider to be intelligence and occupational standing?

I. A DIGRESSION ON INTELLIGENCE

One of the most widely misunderstood concepts is that of intelligence. To begin, let us dispense with one issue immediately. What we call intelligence is "culture specific," i.e., what passes for the signs of intelligence in one cultural milieu will not necessarily be regarded in the same fashion in other cultural settings[3] This is simply to say that the needs of a society define what will be regarded as intelligence in that society. Now, this is not to say that the concept of intelligence is a useless and ephemeral construct, a conclusion that many are prone to accept once the cultural relativity of intelligence is admitted. Quite the contrary. If we admit that it is possible to define a broad set of attributes and skills that are associated with successful functioning within a culture, then intelligence becomes a useful concept. All that is required is some general agreement as to the nature of these skills. Then the task becomes one of measurement of their possession, not so much for the sake of determining where one individual stands relative to another (although this may be important in many contexts), but for the purpose of gaining some insight into the distribution of these attributes within the society. A good deal of concerted effort by psychologists and others has gone into this question of "measuring" intelligence and a number of testing instruments have been developed[4]

Perhaps the most widely known device for intelligence testing is the so-called IQ test[5] It attempts to measure the ability of individuals to perform certain tasks that seem to be generally accepted in Western society as necessary for successful functioning. After widespread use of tests of this sort, it is commonly accepted that the possession of the abilities in question is normally distributed in our society. An example of a distribution of this type is shown in Figure 1. As in standard IQ tests, it is scaled to have a mean of 100 and a standard deviation of about 15. This means that approximately two-thirds of the population would score between 85 and 115 on such a test and 95 percent would score between 70 and 130. Only two-and-one-half percent would be below 70 and another two-and-one-half percent above 130. Tests of this sort have been widely criticized for being "culture bound," i.e., for not truly measuring intelligence, *per se*, but for measuring factors that are a product of an individual's environment. To begin, such criticism suggests that the general concept of intelligence is that it is a physical attribute, just as the ability to perform certain feats of athletic skill presupposes special physical characteristics. This is clearly the case. What we mean by intelligence is a specific set of attributes that are a part of a person's physical endowment. Of course, any attempt at quantifying the possession of these capabilities is suspect, particularly when the results may be used to make comparisons between people or groups of people. However, in the case of standard IQ tests, there is clear evidence that the test items are capable of indicating possession of some broad set of attributes we are willing to call intelligence, independent of the apparent cultural context of the test itself. For example, it is surprising how similar the test items for different cultural groups are. But, we will return to the issue of the validity of the testing devices later.

The apparently physical nature of what is meant by intelligence raises a critical issue for us. If intelligence is a physical characteristic, and, if intelligence is systematically related to economic performance,

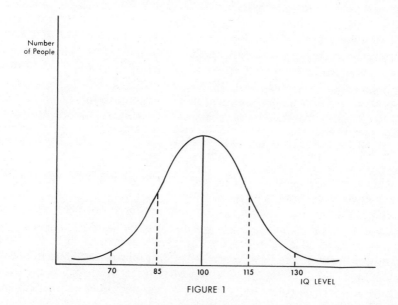

FIGURE 1

what is implied about the origins of inequality in the distribution of human resource type income? The answer would seem to be that inequality has at least some of its roots in physiological differences among people. In certain areas of endeavor, this would be obviously recognized. Take the example alluded to earlier of Henry Aaron's salary as a baseball player. Clearly, in this case, unique physical skills enable Aaron to command an extremely high salary. Now, if intelligence is merely another unique physical skill, shouldn't possession of it also permit one to capture economic rewards in a similar fashion? Turning again to the medical profession for an example, we can reason as follows: Given the demand for doctor's services and the current constraints on entry into medical schools (which ostensibly are based on levels of intelligence, among other things),[6] the available supply of physicians is sufficiently limited to insure their receiving substantial monetary rewards for practicing their profession. In short, large numbers of people are simply automatically eliminated from consideration as potential physicians because of the demands of the calling, just as large numbers of people are almost automatically not considered to be potential professional football, baseball, or basketball players. All individuals are not equal in a physical sense and when society places a substantial importance on a particular physical skill, it may be expected that, in a market economy, those who possess that skill to an unusual degree will be the beneficiaries of society's passion. Since physical skills tend to be normally distributed (intelligence among them), a demand for a high level of aptitude along particular lines rather quickly limits the supply of individuals capable of performing in the necessary fashion. If the minimum aptitude desired is set at just one standard deviation above the average, the population with the necessary qualifications is reduced to one-sixth of the total. In the context of standard intelligence tests, this would mean an IQ of only 115. On the other hand, setting the minimum IQ for being able to perform a particular role at 130 restricts you to about one-fortieth of the total population. Restriction in the supply of a resource of this type operates to create what economists call "economic rent."

II. A SECOND DIGRESSION: THE ROLE OF "ECONOMIC RENT" IN PRODUCING INCOME INEQUALITY

The concept of "economic rent" is a familiar one to economists, involving those situations in which the supply of a factor of production is perfectly inelastic, i.e., changes in the price offered for the factor are incapable of altering the quantity of it offered in the market place. To illustrate this, observe Figure 2. There, we show the hypothetical demand for labor of people with an IQ of 130 or greater. It may seem peculiar to think in terms of a demand for labor with that particular characteristic. In reality, the demand is for people to engage in a number of different occupations that have a range of prerequisites in terms of prior training, etc. For example, certification as a physician involves one set of requirements, as a university professor another, as an engineer another, and so on. However, in a general sense there is a further prerequisite, which is simply the ability, as measured, say, by standard intelligence tests, to acquire the necessary training that constitutes certification. Thus, what we are really talking about is a general demand for a "package" of natural ability and training, with the natural ability component placing a constraint on those who may choose to engage in these activities. Consequently, we may think of the supply of labor of this type as being perfectly inelastic, as shown in Figure 2, for except for growth in population, the number of people with this capacity cannot be increased (assuming, of course, that intelligence is a "physical" trait and is accurately measured by the IQ device).

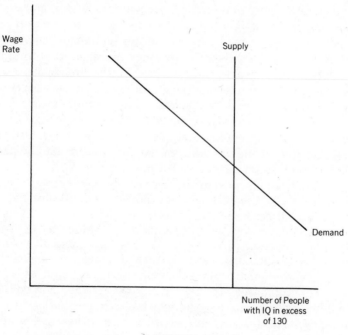

FIGURE 2

The supply inelasticity introduces an element of "economic rent" into the incomes of people with the requisite ability. How much rent depends on the intensity of the demand for their services. The greater the demand, the greater the economic rent, for the nature of economic rent is that it is "price determined" and not "price determining." Thus, the incomes of those who possess the necessary ability are as high as they are because people are willing to pay the prices they do to acquire their services. For example, doctors' incomes are largely what they are because people desire a high level of medical service. Similarly, university professors' salaries rose markedly during the 1960's because the demand for higher education increased substantially in that interval.[7]

Of course, not all the income of people with high levels of intelligence is pure economic rent. Within the group itself, differentials in the degree to which this natural advantage is exploited occur, usually in the form of variations in the amount of specialized training that is acquired. These differentials are then reflected in the amount of income a person can command. He who has engaged in lengthy and expensive training is likely to earn a higher income than he who has not.[8]

III. THE IMPLICATIONS OF "ECONOMIC RENT" FOR THE INHERITANCE OF POVERTY

Returning to our main theme, the heritage of poverty, we may ask what is the significance of our discussions of intelligence and economic rent? Simple. If (1) intelligence is treated as a physical aspect of man and (2) economic rent is paid to those possessing unusual amounts of it, the very real possibility exists that poverty is transmitted from parent to child through the genetic mechanism. In the broadest sense, this implies that poverty is to some substantial extent hereditary in the physical sense. It should be realized, incidentally, that while our argument has been focused primarily on the intelligence factor, the same line of reasoning could be applied to any physical skill that is normally distributed and in sufficient demand to warrant the payment of economic rent (such as unusual athletic ability).

The possibility of physical inheritance of poverty is rarely discussed.[9] Almost exclusively, the thrust of the poverty inheritance hypothesis has been in the direction of emphasizing the importance of features of one's present environment as the driving force behind the inheritance of poverty. The argument runs thusly: (1) The current adult poor live in "deprived" environments because their incomes are low, (2) these "deprived" environments put the children of the poor at an initial disadvantage compared to the children of the non-poor (who, presumably, live in relatively "enriched" environments), and (3) once having fallen behind, the children of the poor never "catch up" with the children of the non-poor and another generation of poor is created.

To be more specific, the environmentalist position focuses heavily on the role that educational opportunity (or lack of it) plays in perpetuating poverty. There is a wealth of evidence that indicates a systematic relationship between observed educational achievement and economic status. This would seem to suggest that a direct attack on poverty can be made by providing the children of the poor with the same *quantity* and *quality* of education as that received by the children of the non-poor. That ought to be simple enough to accomplish. Quantitatively, it is. In fact, some very substantial strides have been made in eliminating educational differences between certain groups in the society, particularly the white-non-white differential.[10] However, that only touches peripherally on the problem. The real crux of the educational differential question is not so much the quantity of education available to the poor but the "quality" of that education.

What do we mean by the "quality" of education? Essentially, quality is measured by the actual performance of students. If students in a school located in a "poor" district do not perform on standardized testing instruments as well as students from non-poor districts, the quality of education is generally deemed to be inferior in the poor district. Attempts to eliminate these "qualitative" differences in education have generated some of the more explosive controversies of recent times. One standard approach to the problem has been to substantially increase the level of per pupil expenditure in the "low quality" districts in an effort to improve student performance. Unfortunately, there is incredibly little evidence to support the premise that pupil performance is sensitive to per pupil expenditures. For example, the general conclusions of the Coleman Report are that there is no relationship between student performance and the volume of resources per pupil committed to public education.[11]

What can explain the apparent lack of impact of per pupil expenditures on student performance? And, what are the implications of this in terms of the inheritance of poverty question? The answer to the first question may simply be that after some expenditure threshold is reached, the critical factor is the native ability (intelligence?) of the student population. If certain physical aptitudes are not present, they cannot be substituted for by increased expenditures. To the second question, the non-sensitivity of educational quality to expenditure levels suggests that attempts at reducing the inheritance of poverty through environmentally improving the "quality" of education available to the poor will not be particularly successful.

The evidence of little relationship between inputs into the public education process and its end product also suggests that the concept of investment in human capital may be overrated as an explanation for individual income differentials. But, how can this be? The relationship between educational accomplishment and income levels is so powerfully strong that investment in human capital in the form of education must have a significant impact on the ability to command income. Not necessarily. It is quite possible that historically both educational accomplishment and income levels have been strongly related to some third factor, namely, the basic intelligence of individuals. This clearly will create the impression of a systematic relationship between education and income, even though the linkage is between ability and income.

Our discussion to this point has strongly emphasized the relationship between individual income levels and the physical attribute we choose to call intelligence. This is not to deny any environmental influences on the determination of the distribution of income in the United States. In particular, it is not to maintain that investment in educational human capital has no impact, especially on the economic returns to selected individuals. However, it is meant to challenge the almost exclusive primacy so commonly assigned to purely environmental influences in discussions of the causes of poverty. This is the "conventional wisdom" alluded to earlier. Interestingly, abandoning the hypothesis of dominance of environmental influences makes a number of puzzling occurrences of recent years a good bit more understandable. For example, the already discussed apparent inability of substantial increases in per pupil expenditures to affect scholastic performance. Or, the apparent failure of various compensatory education programs, such as Head Start, to materially affect the achievement levels of "underprivileged" children.[12] Or, the weak response of the relative income levels of non-white males to the tremendous increases in the relative quantity of non-white education in post-World War II America.

IV. THE HEREDITY vs. ENVIRONMENT ISSUE

Clearly, the basic issue we have raised in this chapter is one of the respective importance of hereditary and environmental factors in influencing the economic performance of individuals. The theme to this point has been that the relative importance of a *physical* attribute, intelligence, in determining people's economic status has consistently been underestimated. The critical point on which the whole argument turns is the physical character of intelligence. We discussed this to a limited extent earlier, but now that the crucial nature of this contention is apparent, it is appropriate that we return to it for a more in depth treatment.

Previously, we pointed out that through devices such as IQ tests, we attempt to measure some set of attributes that we are willing, as a society, to regard as constituting "intelligence." It was also noted that the question of whether the tests used for this purposes were "culture biased" suggested that "intelligence" is conceived to be a physical characteristic of people rather than something that is shaped by their environmental circumstances. This takes us to the truly important issue, namely, are the aptitudes we choose to call intelligence truly physical in character and are we able to obtain measures of those aptitudes that abstract reasonably well from environmental differences among people? These are highly controversial issues for many people, particularly for those who feel that "intelligence testing" constitutes a personal threat to them. However, this does not relieve the need for examining the question: It merely increases it.

While it is difficult to set forth simple answers to these complex questions, we can explore some of their implications that are reasonably testable. To begin, if the thing we call intelligence is truly a set of physical attributes, they should be transmitted from parents to children in a fashion that is predictable from very well established principles of the field of study known as genetics. Therefore, if instruments such as IQ tests do measure this phenomenon with reasonable accuracy, the results of these measurements ought to be predictable from genetic principles in certain controlled situations. Essentially, those situations are ones in which the extent of blood relationship between people as well as their performance on standard IQ tests are known precisely.[14] In such circumstances, it is possible to predict the IQ scores of some individuals from those of others to which they are related by blood. The predicted scores can then be compared with the actual to see how well they "explain" the actual score. Analysis of this sort reveals a striking correspondence between actual IQ scores and those expected on the basis of the known relationship among people. In fact, about 80 percent of the variation in actual IQ scores can be "explained" by the operation of genetic principles of physical heredity.[15] This argues for two propositions: (1) A physical characteristic called "intelligence" does exist and (2) devices such as IQ tests are reasonably capable of measuring it. At the same time, the operation of environmental factors in shaping intelligence is not completely excluded, although their influence is greatly minimized.

V. THE IMPACT OF HEREDITY ON ECONOMIC STATUS

To this point, we have come down rather strongly in favor of explanations of differences in economic status that emphasize physical differences among people. This would clearly suggest that economic status is inheritable, but not quite in the fashion implied in most discussion of this phenomenon. What I have called the conventional wisdom in this respect places the greatest stress on the inheritance of environmental characteristics that give rise to poverty. The differences between the two positions are more than semantic in character. From the standpoint of public policy, they have profoundly different meanings.

On the one hand, the environmental vision of the "cruel legacy of poverty" is one that is replete with opportunities for social engineering in an attempt to alter the character of the contemporary environment of the poor or "prospective poor." By contrast, the view that poverty may to a substantial degree be inherited genetically imposes distinct limits on the extent to which policies aimed at affecting environmental conditions can produce a permanent alteration in the economic status of people. Obviously, this latter view is decidedly less optimistic about the prospects for producing a permanent reduction in the volume of poverty. Also, it clearly argues that a critical determinant in one's economic success is the "genetic package" handed him (or her) at birth. If a person is unfortunate enough to be "underendowed" by the accident of birth, he will bear this handicap all his life. Regrettably, this is all too true. Cruelly so, perhaps, but that does not alter the reality of it one bit.

But, what about the children of those who by genetic accident find themselves severely limited in their capacity to command economic rewards? Are they, too, simply doomed to repeat the experience of their parents? Or, looking at the other side of the picture, are the children of those who have been unusually favored at birth the permanent beneficiaries of nature's largesse? The answer is, "No!" The physical characteristics that may contribute substantially to a person's being in poverty are not passed on from parent to offspring in a rigid one-for-one fashion. Rather, the phenomenon known as "regression towards the mean" operates to moderate the effects of the hereditary mechanism.

Regression towards the mean is rather simply explained. Take "intelligence" as an example. If parents are possessed of either unusually high or unusually low levels of intelligence, their offspring will tend to have intelligence that lies closer to the mean for the population. Thus, the children of extremely intelligent parents tend to be less intelligent than their mother and father, while the children of individuals with very low levels of ability tend to be more gifted than their parents. In effect, nature operates to reduce the extremes in the population.

Given the operation of the principle of regression to the mean, we would expect the tendency for poverty to be inherited to be ameliorated over time. But, considering that there may also be environmental factors working to produce a heritage of poverty, how quickly, if at all, will this take place? Detailed data that would answer this question are not easily found. However, several years ago, information was collected describing the occupations of a sample of men *as well as the occupations of their fathers*. The data are shown in Table 1. They provide some insight into the extent to which one measure of economic achievement, occupational status, is passed from generation to generation. The data shown in Table 1 are not easily interpreted. Looking first at the entries in the table that show the proportion of sons who have the same occupation as their father, there seems to be some tendency toward occupational inheritance. But, how much?

In order to answer that question, we need to ask ourselves how Table 1 would look if (1) there were perfect inheritance of occupations between fathers and sons or (2) there were absolutely no relationship between the occupations of fathers and sons. Perfect inheritance of occupation is easier to describe. This would result in 100 percent of the sons of fathers in each occupation having the same occupation as their father. No inheritance of occupation is somewhat more involved. If this were the case, the occupational distribution of the sons of fathers in any given occupation would be the same as the distribution for all sons. This would result in each row of Table 1 being identical with every other row. In short, sons would be distributed by occupation in exactly

Table 1

DISTRIBUTION OF NONINSTITUTIONAL MALE POPULATION.
25-64 YEARS OF AGE, MARCH 1962,
BY FATHER'S OCCUPATION

Father's Occupation	Son's Occupation									
	Managers, Officials, and Proprietors	Professional, Technical, and Kindred	Craftsmen, Foremen, and Kindred	Sales	Clerical and Kindred	Operatives and Kindred	Service, including Private Household	Laborers, except Farm and Mine	Farmers and Farm Managers	Farm Laborers and Foremen
Managers, officials, and proprietors	0.341	0.216	0.139	0.090	0.070	0.085	0.026	0.019	0.010	0.003
Professional, technical, and kindred	0.175	0.408	0.087	0.090	0.069	0.103	0.030	0.020	0.013	0.004
Craftsmen, foremen, and kindred	0.165	0.130	0.294	0.047	0.078	0.175	0.052	0.048	0.008	0.003
Sales	0.301	0.194	0.119	0.150	0.062	0.104	0.032	0.020	0.017	0.001
Clerical and kindred	0.178	0.281	0.169	0.079	0.096	0.092	0.061	0.031	0.014	0.000
Operatives and kindred	0.122	0.117	0.238	0.044	0.066	0.258	0.060	0.076	0.010	0.010
Service, including private household	0.142	0.101	0.210	0.057	0.095	0.210	0.111	0.062	0.011	0.002
Laborers, except farm and mine	0.080	0.059	0.226	0.037	0.080	0.265	0.091	0.142	0.012	0.012
Farmers and farm managers	0.115	0.053	0.197	0.025	0.047	0.205	0.052	0.085	0.178	0.042
Farm laborers and foremen	0.073	0.023	0.204	0.020	0.038	0.261	0.082	0.134	0.062	0.102

Source: *Current Population Reports, Series P-23*, No. 11, May 12, 1964.

the same fashion irrespective of their father's occupation.

The two extreme cases just described provide benchmarks that can be used to calculate a single index that measures the extent to which inheritance of occupation approaches the case of perfect inheritance.[16] This index would have a value of one if inheritance were complete and zero if there were none. The actual value is 0.40, which suggests some inheritance of economic status but quite a deviation from a perfect transmission from fathers to sons. Interestingly, if the one generation movement shown in Table 1 were to occur for two generations, almost all trace of occupational inheritance disappears (the index of inheritance falls to 0.14).

An alternative way of viewing the impact of inheritance on economic status is provided by the information presented in Table 2. The first column shows 1960 median income levels by occupation, while the

Table 2

MEDIAN INCOME, 1960, AND WEIGHTED AVERAGE MEDIAN INCOME, NONINSTITUTIONAL MALE POPULATION, 25-64 YEARS OF AGE, MARCH, 1962, BY OCCUPATION

Father's occupation	a_j*	Median income 1960	Weighted average median income†
Managers, officials, and proprietors	0.161	$ 6,664	$ 5,747
Professional, technical, and kindred	0.125	6,619	5,735
Craftsmen, foremen, and kindred	0.207	5,240	5,195
Sales	0.051	4,987	5,608
Clerical and kindred	0.066	4,785	5,504
Operatives and kindred	0.189	4,299	4,834
Service, including private household	0.059	3,310	4,833
Laborers, except farm and mine	0.069	2,948	4,686
Farmers and farm managers	0.056	2,169	4,234
Farm laborers and foremen	0.018	1,066	4,021

*Relative importance of occupation among sons.
†Computed using weights for various occupations given in rows of matrix of Table 1.
SOURCE: *U.S. Census, 1960*; Table 5-2, and computations.

second column presents an estimate of the median income of sons according to their father's occupation.[17] If inheritance of occupation were perfect, the two columns would be identical, while if there were no inheritance of occupation, the second column would show a value of $4,907 for all occupations. Thus, with complete inheritance, the range of occupational incomes would be $5,598 and with no inheritance, zero. The actual range is $1,726, which is 31 percent of that which would exist with full inheritance of occupational status. Further, it is interesting to note that in the case of sons of farm laborers and foremen, occupational movement eliminated about three-fourths of the difference between what their income would have been if occupational inheritance were complete and what it would have been with no inheritance ($4,907 — $1,066 or $3,841).[18] Clearly, the actual amount of occupational mobility between generations was sufficient to substantially reduce the income differentials implicit in perfect inheritance of occupation.

VI. CONCLUSIONS

Our discussion has ranged across a rather wide variety of topics: genetics, intelligence testing, educational problems, and economics. What has emerged? Primarily, a view of the process by which poverty is transmitted between generations that places much greater emphasis on the physical inheritance of characteristics that tend to produce poverty. To summarize the basic argument, we commence with the proposition established in the earlier chapters that inequality in the distribution of income (i.e., poverty) must largely be a function of inequality in the distribution of human resource type income. The sources of such inequalities are many, but a major one is the payment of economic rent to individuals possessing unique physical skills that are in great demand within our society. Those skills are inheritable through the genetic mechanism and, consequently, poverty itself may be transmitted in this fashion. Interestingly, an examination of occupational movement between generations suggests that despite the possibility of actual physical inheritance of characteristics that can materially influence economic status, there is a substantial amount of movement between occupations. This would seem to suggest (although it does not prove) that the extent to which economic status is "inherited" through environmental conditions has been overemphasized. Certainly, the difficulties that have frequently been encountered in improving the "quality" of education in "deprived" environments are consistent with such a conclusion.

The intriguing aspect of the view of poverty inheritance expressed here is that it implies an inappropriate focus in many of the public policy approaches to producing long run amelioration of poverty. The overwhelming drift of policy is in the direction of correcting environmental conditions that generate poverty. Commendable, perhaps, but only if the cost of such efforts is commensurate in some manner with the potential gains in terms of poverty reduction. To date, the record in this respect is not one of overwhelming success. At any rate, at the risk of sounding pessimistic, what we have argued here is that the basis of contemporary income inequality in American society may be much more deep seated than many imagine, having some very substantial roots in physiological differences between people. With this as a general background, we will proceed in the next few chapters to assess the economic problems confronting certain minority groups in the society.

FOOTNOTES

[1]*Economic Report of the President, 1964,* Council of Economic Advisers, Washington, D.C., pp. 69-70.

[2]For a discussion of the relationship between mental ability and occupation, see Baer, Max F. and Roeber, Ed. C., *Occupational Information: The Dynamics of Its Nature and Use,* Chicago: Science Research Associates, Inc., Illinois, 1964, pp. 190-195. The most complete ranking of occupations by the ability required to perform them is provided by the *Revised Minnesota Occupational Scales,* Minnesota Studies in Student Personnel Work, No. 2. Minneapolis: University of Minnesota Press, 1953. One of the factors in their ratings is academic ability with four levels being defined:

Level A—upper ten percent of population in abstract intelligence— Professional, semi-professional, and executive employment.

Level B—76th to 90th percentile in abstract intelligence—Technical, clerical, and supervisory employment.

Level C—26th to 75th percentile in abstract intelligence—Skilled tradesmen and low grade clerical workers.

Level D—lowest 25 percent of population in abstract intelligence— Semi-skilled and unskilled employment.

The correspondence between the occupational descriptions, the level of intelligence required, and occupational earnings is evident. One note of caution: These groupings represent average levels of ability. In individual instances, there may be variations. However, our interest is in the averages.

[3]For an excellent discussion of this issue, see Arthur R. Jensen, "How Much Can We Boost IQ and Scholastic Achievement?," *Harvard Educational Review,* Winter 1969, pp. 1-123.

[4]Very sophisticated statistical techniques are used to develop testing instruments capable of measuring an abstract quality known as intelligence. One of the most widely used tools in this respect is factor analysis.

[5]See Jensen, *op. cit.*, for an excellent discussion of the development of the IQ test.

[6]I say "ostensibly based on levels of intelligence" because there is clear evidence of past discrimination in medical school admission practices. In this case, the most striking kind of discrimination is the limiting of the number of Jews admitted in a given class. See Kessel, Reuben, A., "The AMA and the Supply of Physicians," *Law and Contemporary Problems*, Health Care, Pt. 1, Spring 1970, pp. 267-283.

[7]On the other hand, very recently, university professors have not been blessed with substantial salary increases, largely because of an apparent decline in the public demand for higher education.

[8]It should also be recognized that it is possible for a profession to affect the amount of "rent" its members claim by varying the standards of admission to the specialized training that is required. The American Medical Association realizes this all too well and practices supply restriction to accomplish its objective of maintaining high levels of income for physicians.

[9]There may be some contemporary discussion of this idea, but I must admit to not having encountered it.

[10]In October 1952, median school years completed by non-whites was 7.6 and by whites 11.4. As of March 1971, the respective figures were 11.9 and 12.5. Source: *Manpower Report of the President, 1972*, Table B-9.

[11]Coleman, J.S., *et. al.*, *Equality of Educational Opportunity*, Washington, D.C.: United States Office of Education, 1966.

[12]A very thorough discussion of the failure of compensatory education programs is contained in Jensen, *op. cit.*

[13]For evidence on this point, see Harrison, Bennett, "Education and Underemployment in the Urban Ghetto," *American Economic Review*, December 1972, pp. 796-812 and Michelson, Stephan, "Income of Racial Minorities," unpublished doctoral dissertation, Stanford University, 1968.

[14]The standard case is that of identical twins reared in differing environments.

[15]See Jensen, *op. cit.*

[16]Details of calculating this index are provided in my "On the Importance of Picking One's Parents," *Quarterly Review of Economics and Business*, Summar 1966, pp. 7-15.

[17]The estimate is derived by computing a weighted average of incomes for the sons of fathers in a particular occupation where the weights are the entries in the appropriate row of Table 1.

[18]If we adjust the lower income bound to take account of the amount of movement that is necessary to accommodate the reduction in the number of farm laborers over time the proportion of the gap that is eliminated is slightly less than three-fourths (74 percent). Without the adjustment, it is slightly more than three-fourths (77 percent).

RACIAL ASPECTS OF POVERTY

CHAPTER 6

Probably the most deeply emotional aspect of the poverty question has been its differential incidence by race. In its concern with issues of racial equality over the past decade and more, American society has become acutely aware of two things: (1) a substantial income differential between whites and non-whites[1] and (2) a much greater incidence of poverty among non-whites than among whites. The evidence on these points is irrefutable. Table 1 shows non-white income as a fraction of white income for families, males, and females. Perhaps the most critical of these ratios is that for families since it is probably the best indicator of the relative economic position of non-whites as a group. It is now at an historic high, but it is still at a value that is less than two-thirds. Clearly, though, some progress has been made in the post-World War II period in improving the relative income position of non-white families. More will be said about this later.

The statistics describing the relative income position of non-white males and females are extremely interesting because of the great disparity between them. At the beginning of the period for which we have data, the ratio for non-white males was greater than that for females. However, currently, it has fallen substantially behind. This has largely been due to the very rapid improvement in the economic position of non-white women vis-a-vis white women. Again, this will be discussed in more detail at a further point in the chapter.

Table 2 shows rather aptly the impact of the lower income levels of non-whites on the level of poverty found among them. Very consistently, the poverty rate among non-white families has been about two-and-one-half times that for white families. Put another way, the current poverty rate for non-whites is roughly comparable to that for whites at the very beginning of the post-World War II period. This is the crux of the economic problem facing non-whites in the United States.

I. COMPETING EXPLANATIONS OF NON-WHITE ECONOMIC STATUS

There are a number of possible explanations for the differential economic status of whites and non-whites. Placing them in the context of the discussion of the previous chapter, they may be grouped into two categories, environmental and hereditary. The most frequently

Table 1

RELATIVE INCOME OF NONWHITE FAMILIES, NONWHITE MALES, AND NONWHITE FEMALES, UNITED STATES, 1947-70

Year	Relative Income*		
	Families	Males	Females
1947	0.51	n.a.	n.a.
1948	0.53	0.54	0.49
1949	0.51	0.49	0.51
1950	0.54	0.54	0.49
1951	0.53	0.55	0.46
1953	0.57	0.55	0.59
1954	0.51	0.50	0.55
1955	0.56	0.53	0.54
1956	0.53	0.52	0.58
1957	0.54	0.53	0.58
1958	0.51	0.50	0.59
1959	0.52	0.47	0.62
1960	0.55	0.53	0.70
1961	0.53	0.52	0.67
1962	0.53	0.49	0.67
1963	0.53	0.52	0.67
1964	0.56	0.57	0.70
1965	0.55	0.54	0.73
1966	0.60	0.55	0.76
1967	0.62	0.63	0.78
1968	0.63	0.59	0.79
1969	0.63	0.59	0.85
1970	0.64	0.60	0.92

Source: *Current Population Reports, P-60 Series.*

* Ratio of nonwhite to white median income in each group.

n.a.= Not Available.

offered hypotheses as to why non-white incomes are less than those of whites are environmental in nature and revolve about some form of "discrimination" in the society. This "discrimination" can, in turn, be classified as either (1) labor market discrimination or (2) pre-labor

Table 2

PERCENT OF FAMILIES WITH LESS
THAN $3,000 ANNUAL INCOME (1963 PRICES), BY RACE,
UNITED STATES, 1947-1970

Year	Percent of Families with Less than $3,000 Income	
	White	Nonwhite
1947	27.8 %	66.1 %
1950	28.0	62.4
1953	22.7	52.8
1954	24.3	53.6
1955	21.6	51.6
1956	19.4	50.4
1957	19.5	49.8
1958	19.6	51.5
1959	18.2	49.3
1960	18.1	44.9
1961	18.0	46.4
1962	16.8	43.9
1963	15.7	43.1
1964	15.5	37.8
1965	14.5	37.3
1966	13.5	33.2
1967	12.6	31.6
1968	11.1	29.1
1969	10.4	27.1
1970	10.7	27.8

Source: *Current Population Reports, P-60 Series.*

market discrimination. The first of these is what was called
discrimination in Chapter Two and involves employers perceiving the
existence of subjective costs in the hiring of non-white workers.

The second form of discrimination involves the quantity of acquired
human capital that non-whites possess. Most commonly, this takes the
form of a relative lack of formal education on the part of non-whites.
However, it can also include the impact of the general environment
(both social and physical) on the various skills that non-whites bring to
the labor market. Examples of this might be the extent to which the
typical circumstances in which a non-white is reared produce what

employers regard as positive work attitudes or the impact of a "deprived" early environment on the educability of non-whites. The familiar argument in this latter case is that upon entry into the American educational system, non-white children are already disadvantaged and are never able to overcome this handicap.

At this point, we should take note of one other source of the gap between white and non-white income levels, viz., differential access to property income. What this amounts to is a recognition of the fact that non-whites have less wealth than whites. This is shown by the data of Table 3. The magnitude of this wealth differential is perhaps best illustrated by pointing out that the Negro wealth levels shown in Table 3 are roughly the equivalent of those of whites in the United States approximately a full century earlier.[2] Whether these lower non-white wealth levels can be viewed as environmental in nature depends on the view one takes of the source of differentials in human resource type income. Wealth accumulation is largely a product of past income levels and these, for the most part, depend on the receipt of income derived from the sale of human resources.

Table 3

AVERAGE WEALTH OF NEGRO SPENDING UNITS, BY AGE, UNITED STATES, 1953 AND 1962

Age	Average Wealth (Adjusted to 1957-59 Prices)	
	1953	1962
23,24	$ 600	$ 700*
33	1700	1900
43	3100	3500
53	3700	3800
63	4900	4100
73	4100*	3400

Source: Lee Soltow, "A Century of Personal Wealth Accumulation," in *The Economics of Black America*, Harold G. Vatter and Thomas Palm (eds.), Harcourt Brace Jovanovich, Inc., New York, 1972, p. 82. Soltow cites data used by John B. Lansing and John Sonquist, "A Cohort Analysis of Changes in the Distribution of Wealth," in *Six Papers on the Size Distribution of Income and Wealth,* Lee Soltow (ed.), National Bureau of Economic Research, vol. 33, Studies in Income and Wealth. Soltow supplies the asterisked figures as they are not included in the Lansing-Sonquist paper.

So much for the environmental type explanations of the white-non-white income differential. To the extent they are valid, they result in non-whites receiving smaller economic rewards than whites because either (1) they are paid less than whites for the human capital they do possess or (2) they have less in the way of acquired human capital and/or wealth.

But, what about the possibility of non-environmental or hereditary type explanations for the gap between white and non-white income levels? These are rarely discussed in "polite" or sophisticated circles, for what they must ultimately suggest is differential racial endowment with what we have called genetic human capital. The interesting question is why the "hereditary" possibility so seldom receives attention (at least until very recently) in intellectual circles. I suspect the unwillingness to confront this issue stems from a widespread philosophical committment on the part of academics and intellectuals to the concept of a "universal brotherhood of man." Put succinctly, a substantial majority of those who would be expected to consider this issue at the higher levels of intellectual discourse have a profound belief in the desirability of a world in which "color" does not matter, or, for that matter, age, sex, religion, or national background.[3] At the same time, they are very hard pressed to deny the desirability of people being judged on a "merit" basis, precisely because their own position in life is largely regarded as being a function of their own merit.[4] In order to reconcile these views, it is almost mandatory that there be no differences in *group* abilities, as distinguished from *individual* abilities.

Irrespective of the personal philosophic problems that consideration of the "differential hereditary endowment" issue may generate, thoroughness of coverage of our subject dictates its inclusion. This becomes especially apparent when one confronts the actual evidence on this matter. We have already alluded to data that suggest the inheritability of mental ability as measured by standard testing devices. Interestingly, those same tests rather uniformly show differences by race. Specifically, Negroes score about one standard deviation lower than whites on conventional IQ tests.[5] While the evidence in this respect is pervasively consistent, the interpretation of it is quite varied, ranging from positive assertions that there is a genetically rooted differential to equally positive claims that the observed differential can be explained by environmental differences that influence the performance of non-whites on tests of this type.[6]

Why the wide variation in explanations of the observed IQ differential between whites and Negroes? Partly, it undoubtedly reflects philosophical positions such as that discussed earlier or pure and simple prejudice. However, it is entirely possible for men of good will to disagree on this issue due to the difficulty of controlling for environmental factors such as socio-economic status. For example, if socio-economic status itself is a function of genetic human capital (as suggested earlier), controlling for differences in the socio-economic status of those receiving an IQ test may be largely a tautological exercise. For example, if a group of school children are being tested, statistically controlling for the income level of their parents will bias the white-Negro comparison in the direction of showing similar IQ's *if* (1) the economic status of the parents depends functionally on their IQ and (2) IQ is inheritable.

Given these difficulties, is it possible to develop any evidence on this question? Yes, if we proceed inferentially. What we know at this point is that there is evidence of inheritability of IQ through the genetic mechanism among the population in general. This increases the likelihood that the observed white-Negro IQ differential is of genetic origin. Beyond this, there is some interesting evidence in a study by Gerald Lesser, *et. al.*, that strongly indicates the presence of differences in the nature of the mental ability of various racial and/or ethnic groups *independent of socio-economic status.* The Lesser analysis deals with the performance of pre-literate school children from four different ethnic/racial groups: Jewish, Chinese, Negroes, and Puerto Ricans. Children are selected in a fashion to permit controlling for socio-economic status and are then tested for four types of mental skills: verbal, reasoning, numerical, and spatial. Great care seems to have been taken in the testing process to avoid the common pitfalls associated with the testing of children.[8]

A graphic summary of the Lesser results is shown in Figures 1 and 2 with Figure 1 depicting mean test scores for lower class children and Figure 2 mean test scores for middle class children. The results are revealing in two respects. First, there are obvious differences in the *levels* of the group scores within socio-economic class. Jewish children score the highest,[9] followed by Chinese, Puerto Ricans, and Negroes. This is consistent with the existence of genetic differences in endowment, but there is still the possibility that uncontrolled environmental factors operate to produce these results. Therefore, we approach these findings cautiously. The second, and perhaps most important, result shown by the Lesser study is the *variation* in the *pattern* of scores for the different mental aptitudes. Clearly, some groups are relatively more facile in the verbal area, others in the numerical, etc. And, *most interesting*, the patterns are clearly independent of socio-economic status. For each of the four ethnic/racial groups, very similar (in fact, almost identical) patterns of variation in test scores are found among both lower and middle class children.

What is the significance of this evidence? Essentially, it renders it more difficult to account for observed group differences in scores on mental aptitude tests by recourse to environmental explanations. To reconcile this evidence with the non-genetic hypothesis requires that (1)

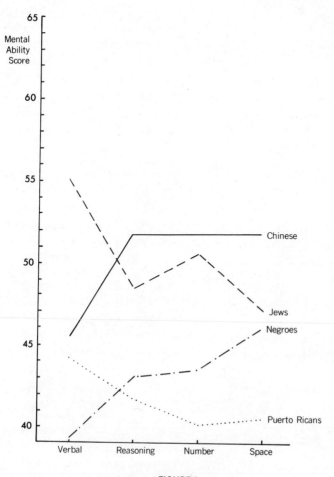

FIGURE 1

Patterns of Normalized Mental Ability
Scores for Lower Class Children,
by Race and Ethnic Group

there be imperfect control for either socio-economic status or other environmental influences and (2) environmental factors other than socio-economic status impact differentially on the various ethnic/racial groups. The necessity of both of these conditions being met in order to justify the environmental position is straightforward. Any admission that *patterns* of variation in test scores are the product of non-environmental circumstances seriously compromises the contention that *differences* in the average level of such scores are environmentally determined. After all, if there are genetically produced differentials in performance on different portions of an overall mental test, why not genetic differentials in overall performance?

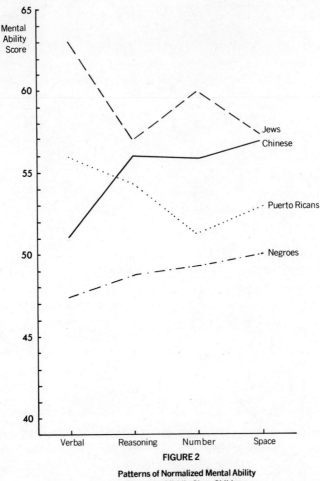

FIGURE 2

**Patterns of Normalized Mental Ability
Scores for Middle Class Children,
by Race and Ethnic Group**

In all honesty, we cannot rule out the possibility that the necessary conditions for confirming the environmental hypothesis are satisfied. However, as we more specifically define what those conditions are, we reduce the range of circumstances that are compatible with environmentalism. In a world of imperfect knowledge, this imposes greater demands on one's capacity for faith, for that is essentially what we seem to be discussing. If one has sufficient faith in the environmental position, most conflicting evidence can be explained away by resort to negativistic propositions to the effect that the environmental hypothesis has not been "disproven" because of "imperfections" in the data or the "research design." For that matter, it could be argued in the other direction that the genetic hypothesis has not been proven or disproven for the same reasons. However, since the conventional wisdom is environmental, differential standards of proof seem to be the order of the day. I must admit that, at times, environmental reasoning reminds me of the American Tobacco Institute's response to the Surgeon General's report on the relationship between cigarette smoking and various types of disease: strained and nit-picking.

Perhaps the best way to illustrate the problem we confront at this juncture is to engage in a minor digression on the nature of empirical "proof" of hypotheses.[10] Actually, we never produce empirical evidence that conclusively proves a hypothesis. Conclusive "proofs" (i.e., those that have a probability of being correct of 1.0) only exist in the shape of formal exercises in logic. In the hurly-burly world of empirical testing of questions, the best we can say is that evidence either is or is not compatible with a hypothesis. Empirical evidence does not prove or disprove hypotheses. It merely gives us greater or lesser reason for accepting or rejecting them.[11] This is because, by their very nature, hypotheses (if properly stated) can never be "conclusively" proven or disproven since they incorporate the concept of "causation" and "causation" is a metaphysical concept not susceptible to empirical proof.

If we grant that hypotheses cannot be "proven" or "disproven," what can we say about them and what standards govern what we say? As already noted, all that we can do is state that the empirical evidence is consistent with or inconsistent with a hypothesis. And, frequently, we may have to say that under certain conditions it may be consistent with more than one hypothesis. This is precisely the case we face here. Much of the available evidence can be construed as being consistent with both the environmental or genetic hypotheses. In these circumstances, what standards does one use in discriminating between alternative hypotheses? In an ideal world, the available evidence is weighed and an informed judgment is made in as objective a fashion as possible. Simple, isn't it? Not quite!

To begin, there is a delicate problem of weighing and assessing various types of evidence and arriving at some judgment as to its total meaning. This can be particularly difficult in the social sciences where our data are frequently exceedingly imperfect. Of necessity, there is some intrusion of one's own attitudes into the judgmental process and the possibility of bias arises. The only safeguards against bias entering into one's own thinking are continual introspective probing of one's own thought processes and repeated testing of ideas in the intellectual market place. The latter is particularly effective if the world of ideas is emotionally neutral with respect to the hypotheses under consideration. Unfortunately, in the particular case we are discussing, it is debatable whether this neutrality exists. For example, in response to a straightforward statement by Arthur Jensen arguing for further research on and testing of the genetic hypothesis, the National Academy of Science demurred on the grounds of the controversial character of the hypothesis.[12] Part of the rationale for such a position is that discussing the hypothesis openly has great potential for generating social unrest. Consequently, it may be "socially irresponsible" to even consider the possibility that the genetic hypothesis is valid. This is an interesting line of reasoning; remarkably similar to that invoked by the Roman Catholic Church in response to the potentially disruptive ideas of Galileo and, certainly, little different from the rationale advanced by authorities in the Soviet Union to justify the supression of intellectual activity. The truly unusual aspect of this argument is that it does not emanate from a source of religious or political authority (which might be expected), but from within the academic community itself.

Given the generally non-neutral attitudes of the intellectual milieu concerning the genetic hypothesis, the path of least resistance is to simply accept the environmental position. There are attractive reasons for doing this. It is consistent with certain widely held philosophic positions within the intellectual community and it leads rather naturally toward policy prescriptions that are popular among academics, such as increased expenditures for educational purposes. Clearly, the opportunities for social engineering are substantially greater if problems are environmental in nature and, very frankly, most social scientists are frustrated social engineers.

By this time, though, it must be obvious that my own choice after considering the available evidence leans strongly toward the genetic hypothesis. On what basis is that choice made? Simply this. I ask myself what I would do if some bizarre individual had the power to (1) force me to choose between the validity of the genetic and environmental hypotheses[13] and (2) to impose a substantial penalty on me if I answered incorrectly. It is assumed that he knows the correct answer and will be honest in informing me whether I have responded properly. Under those circumstances, there is simply no opportunity to hedge one's views. Admittedly, answering such a hypothetical question is a somewhat "iffy" proposition. Nevertheless, I strongly feel that if confronted with such a situation, I would elect the genetic hypothesis.[14]

II. THE ECONOMIC SIGNIFICANCE OF THE GENETIC HYPOTHESIS

Suppose that the hypothesis of genetic differentials in mental aptitudes is valid. What is the significance of such a conclusion from the standpoint of the distribution of income within the United States? Essentially, it suggests differential racial endowments of genetic human capital and differential capacity to command the economic rent that accrues to it. From the perspective of those who wish to hire labor (i.e., employers), variations in the amount of genetic human capital possessed by different types of labor will be reflected in differential levels of productivity. If employers act in a maximizing fashion, this implies that the labor possessing less genetic human capital will be paid less due to its lower productive capacity. This assumes, of course, that genetic human capital enters directly into a firm's production function as a factor of production. Therefore, if the genetic hypothesis has meaning in an economic context, we would expect to find (1) differential levels of productivity between white and Negro labor and (2) differential rewards to white and Negro labor that reflect these productivity differentials.

Some limited evidence is available that is consistent with the economic implications of the genetic hypothesis. To fully understand that evidence, it must be realized that there is more than one way in which employers might respond to the existence of racial differentials in levels of genetic human capital. On the one hand, they might simply choose to integrate their labor force only to the extent that levels of genetic human capital would be similar for whites and Negroes. This would create a situation in which Negroes would be relatively excluded from employment and there would be no productivity differentials between whites and Negroes except for those produced by variations in the quantities of non-genetic human capital and physical capital available to these workers. Further, in the absence of discrimination against Negroes, there would be no white-Negro wage differential.

The alternative mode of adjustment would be to employ Negroes in quantities that exceed those that would produce equal levels of genetic human capital by race and pay Negroes less by an amount sufficient to compensate employers for the lower levels of productivity this would produce. Obviously, if employers, in addition, practice wage discrimination against Negroes, the actual white-Negro wage differential will exceed that warranted by the productivity differences.

An examination of data taken from the Census of Manufactures and the decennial Census of Population reveals relationships that correspond to those just described. Specifically, in manufacturing industries in which there is relative exclusion of non-white labor, there is no significant relationship between either wage levels or average output per worker and the proportion of employment that is non-white. On the other hand, in manufacturing industries in which there is no exclusion of non-whites, both wage and productivity levels are negatively related to the proportion of the work force that is non-white. *In all cases, the quantity of both physical capital and non-genetic human capital of the educational variety has been controlled for in the analysis.*[15] It is also interesting to note that the wage differential associated with the employment of non-white labor is almost exactly that which would be predicted on the basis of the productivity differential.[16] This would suggest the absence of pure wage discrimination on the part of manufacturing employers.

Admittedly, these data pertain only to a limited portion of the American economy, manufacturing employment. Nevertheless, they are remarkably consistent with the economic implications of the genetic hypothesis. Further, the absence of evidence of pure wage discrimination suggests the possibility that existing white-non-white economic differentials are essentially the product of differentials in productive capacity that are unrelated to education (this has been held constant in the anlysis). Can this be? To explore this possibility, let us assume that there is some close relationship between economic status and the conventional measures of mental capacity.[17] Now, the latter are normally distributed while income distributions tend towards being log normal in character. What this implies is a straightforward transformation between the mental ability and income distributions.

To illustrate the possible nature of this relationship, we will employ the standard IQ distribution with mean of 100 and standard deviation of 15 and show how it can be transformed into the present income distribution. The distribution of family income shown in Chapter Three (Table 1) will be used for this purpose. As a first step, both the various income levels and IQ's are expressed as a fraction of their respective medians. Due to the normality of the IQ distribution, its median is equal to the mean of 100. Next, for example, we know from the income distribution that 4.6 percent of families and unrelated individuals had incomes in excess of $25,000 in 1970. Let us assume for the moment that these are also the top 4.6 percent of the IQ distribution. Since we know the character of the IQ distribution (normal), it can be calculated that an IQ of at least 125 would be necessary to place one in the upper 4.6 percent of the distribution. The $25,000 income boundary is approximately two-and-one-half times the median income level, while an IQ of 125 translates into 1.25 times its median. A simple calculation reveals that 2.5 is approximately equal to 1.25 raised to the fourth power. In fact, if similar calculations are made for all the income boundaries of the personal income distribution shown in Chapter Three, it appears that the following relationship roughly holds:

(1) $[Y_b/Y_m] = [M_b/100]^4$

for any percentage of the population, where Y_b and M_b represent the respective lower income and IQ boundaries which separate that fraction of the population from the remainder and Y_m is the median income level. Figure 3 shows graphically the calculated values for each lower income boundary as well as the relationship defined in expression (1). The approximate correspondence is quite clear.

A word of clarification at this point. In order to make the calculations depicted graphically in Figure 3, we have assumed a strict one to one ordering between the income and IQ distributions. Clearly, this would not exist in reality. However, all that is really required for this analysis to be useful is a significant degree of relationship between the two distributions.[18] This does not seem to be an unreasonable assumption.[19] Granting this, what is the significance of our discussion for the problem at hand, *viz.*, the relationship between white and Negro economic status? Simply this: The available evidence suggests a one standard deviation difference between white and Negro IQ's, the bulk of which is the result of genetic factors.[20] Thus, after taking account of the portion

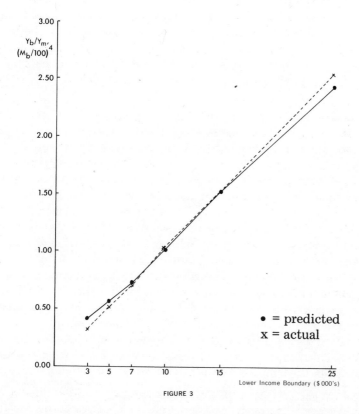

FIGURE 3

of the IQ differential that may be explained by environmental factors, a residual genetically produced differential of perhaps 10 to 12 points might remain. This means the median adjusted IQ for Negroes would be about 88 or 90. For the white population, we will assume a median IQ of 100.

Substituting the median IQ values into expression (1) yields interesting results. Obviously, in the case of whites, the calculated value of Y_b / Y_m is unity which indicates that Y_b is equal to the median income level. For non-whites, though, the calculated value of Y_b / Y_m lies in the range of .60 to .65 suggesting that the median income level for Negroes would be about 60 to 65 percent of that of whites, *solely because of the difference in the quantity of genetic human capital they possess.* Interestingly, this is very close to the actual ratio of Negro to white income in very recent years. The possible implications of this are somewhat staggering. We noted earlier that while there had been progress in the post-World War II era in closing the white-Negro income gap, the remaining differential is still huge. This is particularly disquieting, considering the tremendous strides made in improving the relative education levels of Negroes in these years. Given the great progress along these lines, more substantial improvement in the relative income position of Negroes might have been expected, unless, and this is the critical point, there is some upper limit on the ratio of Negro to white income that is imposed by differential endowments of genetic human capital. If this is the case and if we are approaching that limit, further progress in improving the relative income position of Negroes may be painfully slow.

While this argument may be consistent with the behavior of the relative income levels of Negro families and Negro males, what about the tremendous improvement in the income position of Negro females vis-a-vis white females? Isn't this evidence that environmental factors such as discrimination against Negroes are operative in our society? Further, doesn't it suggest that these factors can be manipulated and controlled? Perhaps, but not necessarily. To begin, women in general do not appear able to capture economic rent on genetic human capital to the same extent as men (this will be treated in detail in the next chapter). Female income levels are approximately one-half those of males. Since there is no evidence of differential *levels* of endowment with genetic human capital (as we have treated it thus far) by sex, this would seem to suggest a substantial degree of underemployment of female labor. Put another way, many women appear to be over-qualified, in terms of their genetic human capital, for the tasks they perform. This opens up an interesting avenue of employer adjustment to private and social pressures for equal employment opportunity.

Consider the situation facing many employers who must submit detailed reports to the federal government describing the racial and sexual composition of their labor force as well as respond to private pressures to hire minority groups. Assume, in the case of Negroes, that hiring more minority group members means, on the average, less genetic human capital among their labor force. Under such conditions, what is the optimal (or cost minimizing) method of adjusting to these pressures? Simple. If women are generally over-qualified genetically for their employment, much of the genetic human capital they possess is irrelevant to their jobs. Therefore, it may be relatively costless to employers to hire Negro females. Given the tendency in recent years towards emphasizing equal employment opportunity for women, this may be doubly advantageous as it, so to speak, "kills two birds with one stone." In short, perhaps the simplest and cheapest way for employers to respond to the multiple pressures they face on the minority group employment front is to hire Negro women. In some respects, this group may be capturing economic rent because of their "Negroeness" and sex. This would explain the dramatic improvement in their relative income position.

III. CONCLUSIONS

Let us be clear as to the major conclusion of this discussion. The thrust of our argument has been that a major source of the white-Negro income gap is probably differential endowments of genetic human capital. This is a conclusion with powerful implications, particularly in the area of public policy. Obviously, it poses a major challenge to the present orientation of policy in the anti-poverty and equal opportunity areas, whether that policy be enunciated through formal legislation or through court decisions. Two major themes have dominated the public discussion of these matters in recent years: (1) the need for both quantitative and qualitative improvements in relative levels of Negro education and (2) the necessity for employers to abandon their patterns of discrimination against Negroes. Such a policy emphasis suggests that (1) education differentials exist and (2) there are income differentials that cannot be explained on the basis of variations in the quantity of education received by Negroes and whites. The most recent evidence indicates that this is precisely the case. From Table 4, it can be seen that for Negro males aged 25 years and over, the distribution by educational class indicates less formal education among Negroes than among whites. Further, within the various educational classes, the average income level of Negroes is consistently less than that for whites.

The evidence shown in Table 4 has conventionally been interpreted as being indicative of both discrimination in the provision of education and wage discrimination against Negroes. However, this presumes the validity of the environmental explanations for the observed racial differences in mental ability. What if, as we have argued, these are probably produced by genetic differences? Can this possibility be reconciled with the data of Table 4? Interestingly, it can. In fact, in some respects, it explains the patterns of wage differentials more satisfactorily than the environmental-discrimination hypothesis. One very perplexing aspect of that hypothesis is the apparently greater degree of discrimination against Negroes with the most education (those with some college) than against Negroes with the least education (those with either none or an elementary level exposure). In the context of the environmental-discrimination thesis, this implies that

Table 4

MEAN INCOME, MALES 25 YEARS AND
OLDER, BY RACE AND EDUCATION
UNITED STATES, 1970

Educational Level	White Male		Negro Male		Ratio of Negro to White Income
	Number (000's)	Mean Income	Number (000's)	Mean Income	
Elementary School	11,801	$5,434	1,973	$3,882	.714
High School	21,793	8,903	2,027	6,124	.687
College	12,732	13,118	486	8,722	.665
Total	46,327*	9,185	4,486	5,429	.591

Source: *Current Population Reports, P-60 Series.*

* Total does not equal sum of parts due to rounding.

discrimination in the market place *increases with education.* This simply does not square with certain conceptualizations of the sources of discrimination in the United States. Take, for example, what, for lack of a better name, I call the Archie Bunker syndrome. This maintains that the prejudice that gives rise to discrimination has its roots in the working class mentality which (1) has difficulty accepting anyone who is "different" and (2) views Negroes as a direct economic threat. It is further argued that the effect of education on attitudes such as these can only be salutary since it operates to destroy prejudice through exposing people to the "pure light of reason." The epitome of this line of thinking is the rather frequent descriptions of middle and lower socio-economic groups in derisive terms, such as "red-neck" or "hard-hat," for example. Or, the recent tendency to impute racist attitudes to so-called "ethnic" groups. Or, the frequent characterization of trade unions as major producers of discrimination. Of course, the corollary of this proposition is that the relatively educated constitute an "elite" that is not infected with the virus of racial prejudice.

Clearly, the Archie Bunker syndrome is not supported by the evidence shown in Table 4. Admittedly, it could be argued that those with greater amounts of education do not exercise control over the hiring practices of their employers. To a certain degree, this is perhaps true. However, in many instances where specialized training is involved, some type of professional judgment is required before a person is hired and this judgment is most likely to be made by someone with equivalent levels of education. Thus, if discrimination is less prevalent among the more educated, there ought to be evidence of it in the data we have presented.

There are two possible explanations for the anomaly of lower relative incomes for Negroes with greater education. First, it is possible that discrimination is more marked at higher educational levels. In all honesty, though, this is a difficult hypothesis to accept. There is strong evidence to suggest positive correlations between one's level of education and the "liberalness" of his political philosophy as well as "liberalness" and the desire not to discriminate on the basis of color.[21] Therefore, I am inclined to reject the simple discrimination hypothesis. The second explanation for the data of Table 4 builds on the differential endowment of genetic human capital thesis. Assume that (1) there is a significant positive relationship between the quantity of education received and mental ability as conventionally measured and (2) approximately a one standard deviation differential between white and Negro scores on mental ability tests. From Table 4, we know that 27.5 percent of white males have some college education. If these 27.5 percent were from the top of the white male IQ distribution, the minimum IQ required for inclusion in this "elite" group would lie 0.66 standard deviations above the mean. From the assumption of a one standard deviation difference between white and Negro IQ's, we know that the minimum IQ to qualify a Negro male for this group would lie 1.66 standard deviations above the mean for Negroes. Since IQ's are normally distributed, this means that approximately 4.9 percent of Negro males would have at least this IQ level. However, as we can clearly see from Table 4, 10.8 percent of Negro males over age 25 have some college education. What this suggests is the possibility that Negro males with college education possess, on the average, *less* genetic human capital than white males with similar education levels.[22]

Extending this analysis to the other two educational groups produces the results shown in Table 5 where the predicted number of Negro males in each educational class is calculated as previously described. An examination of the data shown in Table 5 indicates that the greatest *relative* discrepancy between the predicted and actual proportion of Negro males in the various educational groups (measured by the ratio of the actual to the predicted proportion) occurs among those with some college education. This is precisely where the greatest discrimination occurs. The implication is clear: If our assumptions are valid, Negro males with some college education probably have less genetic human capital *relative* to their white counterparts than Negro males with less education. This could well account for the puzzling existence of an apparent positive relationship between educational level and

Table 5

ACTUAL AND PREDICTED DISTRIBUTION OF MALES 25 YEARS OF AGE AND OLDER, BY EDUCATIONAL CLASS AND RACE, ASSUMING ONE STANDARD DEVIATION DIFFERENTIAL IN MENTAL ABILITY BETWEEN WHITES AND NEGROES, UNITED STATES, 1970

Educational Class	Percent of all Whites in Class	Percent of all Negroes in Class	Predicted Percent of all Negroes in Class	Ratio of Actual Percent Negro to Predicted Percent Negro
Elementary School	25.5	44.0	62.2	0.71
High School	47.0	45.2	32.9	1.37
College	27.5	10.8	4.9	2.20

Source: *Current Population Reports, P-60 Series.*

discrimination against Negroes. In fact, it is intriguing to note the very precise relationship between the ratio of Negro to white income and the ratio of the actual number of Negroes in an educational class to the predicted number.

One further comment before closing. Obviously, what we have argued in this chapter does not reflect favorably on one of the most widely advocated policy approaches to the problem of racial economic differences, *viz.*, increased formal education for Negroes. If we are correct, increasing the proportion of Negroes receiving higher education will probably result in an intensification of the frustration of Negro expectations. The reason for this is that they will be disappointed in the "apparent" economic return to their education since they will not be able to capture economic rent on genetic human capital to the same degree as whites with similar educational levels. Among advocates of the environmental hypothesis, this will be widely interpreted as further evidence of the pervasiveness of "discrimination." Yet, to avoid this problem probably involves widely differing proportions of whites and Negroes receiving higher education. For example, the data of Table 5 indicate that this dilemma could be avoided only at the expense of the proportion of whites attending college being over five times greater than the proportion of Negroes. In the contemporary social milieu, this is unthinkable.[23] Therefore, what we can probably expect is a continuation of the pattern of the past several years, namely, dissatisfaction among Negroes arising out of their being disappointed with the economic benefits that accrue to them in the "white man's world."

FOOTNOTES

[1]The bulk of non-whites in the United States are Negroes. Thus, the problem is essentially a white-Negro income differential. Historically, though, information is more readily available on a non-white basis.

[2]See Lee Soltow, "A Century of Personal Wealth Accumulation," in *The Economics of Black America*, Harold G. Vatter and Thomas Palm (eds.). New York: Harcourt Brace Jovanovich, Inc., 1971. pp. 80-84.

[3]An excellent treatment of this point is provided in Fein, Leonard J., *The Ecology of the Public Schools*. New York: Pegasus, 1971, Chapter Two.

[4]There are few academicians who would be willing to concede that their local service station attendant, for example, is as qualified, either by training or ability, as they to perform the function of determining what should be taught and how it should be taught in their classroom. Admittedly, many of them would be willing to assign that responsibility to a seventeen year old freshman: However, not all behavior, even that of academics, need be consistent.

[5]A brief survey of this evidence is presented in Jensen, "Can We Boost IQ and Scholastic Achievement?," *op. cit.* A point of clarification: Jensen simply states that there is sufficient evidence of racial differences in IQ to warrant considering the hypothesis that they are of genetic origin. In his quite controversial article, he is extremely circumspect on this point. He does not argue that the hypothesis has been proven, but does contend that it ought to be researched more thoroughly than is currently being done. For balance, one should also read "Discussion: How Much Can We Boost IQ and Scholastic Achievement?," *Harvard Educational Review*, Spring 1969, pp. 273-356.

[6]I would place Jensen midway on this spectrum.

[7]Lesser, Gerald S., Fifer, Gordon, and Clark, Donald H., *Mental Abilities of Children from Different Social Class and Cultural Groups*, Volume 30, Monographs of the Society for Research in Child Development. Chicago: University of Chicago Press, 1965.

[8]For example, the tests were administered by individuals with ethnic or racial backgrounds similar to those of the children in order to minimize communications and language difficulties.

[9]The apparent superior mental abilities of Jews was noted recently in a lecture in London by the noted writer C.P. Snow. Interestingly, when asked by reporters in a post-lecture interview what his reaction was to Arthur Jensen's article, he remarked to the effect that Jensen should be more careful in making such statements. Considering Jensen's circumspection in making claims for genetic differences in mental ability and Snow's lack of it, his comments are remarkable, to say the least.

[10]What follows is essentially an argument for what has been called "logical positivism."

[11]Our remarks here imply that hypotheses are stated positively and either accepted or rejected. This is somewhat the academic convention in Economics. However, in the strict sense of things, what we do is state what statisticians call the "null" hypothesis, namely, that no significant relationship or differences exist. We then either accept or reject that hypothesis. Rejection of the "null" hypothesis "suggests" acceptance of the positive hypothesis but is not as strong a statement of affirmation of such a hypothesis.

[12]At a meeting of the National Academy of Sciences at Dartmouth College in September 1969, a letter was read stating the National Academy's decision not to support recommendations urging the study of the link between intelligence and genetic factors.

[13]By the "genetic" hypothesis, we mean the position that genetic differences are the primary (but not necessarily exclusive) source of differentials in individual intelligence (as measured, say, by the IQ testing instrument).

[14]To help allay the suspicion that this may reflect nothing more than a long term "racist" bias on my part, I would recommend to the reader some of my earlier writings. In particular, see "The Anatomy of the Negro-White Income Differential," in *The Negro and Employment Opportunity*, H.R. Northrup and R.L. Rowan (eds.). Ann Arbor: Bureau of Industrial Relations, University of Michigan, 1965, pp. 45-64, and "The Negro and Poverty," *Journal of Business*, January 1967, pp. 27-35. The views expressed in those articles are quite consistent with what I have called "the conventional wisdom."

[15]The precise results are contained in Gallaway, Lowell E., and Scully, Gerald W., "An Economic Analysis of Minority Group Discrimination," Midwest Economic Association, Chicago, Illinois, April 1969. Portions of them are reported in *Manpower Economics, op. cit.*, Chapter 11. Control for the quantities of other types of capital is produced by including in the pertinent regression equations variables that take into account the ratio of acquired human capital to labor and the ratio of physical capital to labor.

[16]On the average, the hourly wage rate in these industries constituted about 30 percent of the value of average output per man hour. The wage differential referred to was almost exactly equal to 30 percent of the productivity differential.

[17]Three recent investigations provide evidence to support such a relationship. First, Taubman, P. and Wales, T., "Higher Education, Mental Ability, and Screening," *Journal of Political Economy*, January/February 1973, p. 35, conclude that "it is almost certain that for those who are at least high school graduates, ability is a more important determinant of the range of income distribution than is education." Second, in a longitudinal study of Swedish citizens, P. de Wolff and A.R.D. van Slijpe, "The Relation between Income, Intelligence, Education, and Social Background," European Meeting of the Econometric Society, Budapest, Hungary, September 1972, find that intelligence is an important determinant of income, but not as strong a one as implied by Taubman and Wales. Finally, Christopher Jencks, in his controversial new book, argues the same position as Taubman and Wales. See *Inequality; A Reassessment of the Effect of Family and Schooling in America*. New York: Basic Books, 1972.

[18]Random variations associated with individual personal characteristics will obviously enter into the relationship. Thus, some people may be placed more highly in the income distribution than their IQ would seem to warrant and some may be placed too low. Over a sizable range, this randomness may be canceled out by an averaging effect. However, at the extremes this will not be as likely to happen.

[19]The reader is referred to the citations of footnote 17. I have been citing Jencks' work as providing support for my position. In all fairness to him, I should point out that he would not put the same interpretation on his results that I have. He assigns a dominant role in explaining income differences to "residual" factors. For example, he would state that IQ variations will account for about 12 percent of the variance in individual income levels, leaving 88 percent to be explained by other factors. This is true at the *individual* level. However, at the group level, which is our primary interest, the proportion of explained variance will be much greater. This is due to the grouping of people resulting in a reduction in the "noise" introduced into the relationship between IQ and income by interpersonal variations in characteristics that affect individual performance. With broad groups, the range of such interpersonal variation is fairly similar and, thus, examining group behavior enables us to abstract from that source of variation. I have worked with both group and individual data and my experience suggests rather strongly that a variable that performs as well as IQ in explaining individual variations in income levels will be very powerful in accounting for inter-group variations in income levels. Consequently,

I regard the 12 percent of individual income differences explained by the data Jencks cites as indicating a strong relationship between income and intelligence. For a very readable summary of Jencks' position, see Bane, Mary Jo and Jencks, Christopher, "Five Myths About Your IQ," *Harper's*, February 1973, pp. 28ff.

[20] See Jensen, *op. cit.*

[21] In all fairness, one should note an alternative explanation of the apparent contradiction between personal philosophy and performance by those with greater levels of education, namely, that "racism" is so all pervasive in the society that people are not even aware that they are infected by it. Unfortunately, this is not a testable hypothesis since there is no possible combination of evidence that will refute it. It is merely an assertion based on faith (or lack of it).

[22] The alternative hypothesis, pure discrimination, yields some interesting implications. If there are no racial differences in genetic human capital, on the average, Negroes with some college education ought to have *more* genetic human capital (not less) than whites with some college education. This being the case, the observed greater discrimination against this group is even more significant in meaning. That is something to ponder. Further, as a matter of evidence, one is entitled to ask the question whether Negroes who have attended college have, on the average, more ability than their white counterparts. This would support the pure discrimination hypothesis.

[23] There is clearly some tendency on the part of colleges and universities to indulge in the practice of racial quotas in admissions. This will insure a continuance of present levels of relative Negro college enrollment and will probably lead to its increasing.

POVERTY AMONG WOMEN

After the rather grim analysis of the preceding chapter, it is almost a relief to approach the subject of the incidence of poverty among women, not because the problems are any less complex or the issues less important, but because the answers we obtain more closely approach the conventional and are probably (although not clearly) much less controversial. Let us commence with an overview. How much poverty is there among women compared to men? To answer that question, we must distinguish between different groups of women. On the one hand, we have women who are members of a family unit but are not regarded as the head of a household. Ignoring the question of how income is distributed within families, it would seem that the economic status of these women is synonomous with that of their family unit. At least, the question of their poverty status is determined by the family level of income rather than by their own personal income level. Admittedly, this may seem to gloss over the question of whether working women (particularly working wives) are discriminated against in the labor market. However, we shall ultimately deal with that issue. For now, though, our interest will be primarily in the economic position of women who are functioning as heads of family units.

I. POVERTY LEVELS AMONG FEMALE FAMILIES

Table 1 presents some simple poverty rates for families that have a woman as the head of the household. The data are for the post-World War II period in the United States and employ the standard definition of poverty that we have used throughout this book. For comparison purposes, the poverty rate for all families is also provided. Just a cursory examination of these poverty rates reveals that the poverty rate for families headed by a woman has behaved quite differently from that for all families. The all family rate shows the previously noted steady and persistent tendency to decline. On the other hand, the poverty rate for families with a female head declined hardly at all between the end of World War II and 1959 and then commenced to fall in a reasonably steady fashion, although not as rapidly as the overall poverty rate. For example, the 1947 and 1959 poverty rates for families headed by a woman are 50.1 and 51.3 percent, respectively. However, since 1959, that rate has fallen by about one-fourth. During the same period, the all family poverty rate fell by about 40 percent. It is also worth noting that the current poverty rate among families with a female head is almost three times as large as that for all families.

The gap between the poverty rate for families headed by a woman and the general poverty rate has two interesting dimensions. First, there is the question of why there is a differential burden of poverty for these families. The most obvious answer to that question is that income levels are lower for families in this category. True, but this is a somewhat superficial reply. The really basic issue is why income levels

Table 1

PERCENT OF FAMILIES WITH FEMALE
HEAD WITH LESS THAN $3,000 INCOME
IN 1963 PRICES, UNITED STATES,
1947-70

Year	Percent with Less than $3,000 Income
1947	50.1
1948	56.2
1949	54.7
1950	58.7
1951	54.9
1952	56.0
1953	52.4
1954	55.1
1955	52.3
1956	48.7
1957	49.8
1958	51.0
1959	51.3
1960	48.8
1961	49.0
1962	47.5
1963	47.1
1964	44.2
1965	43.7
1966	40.5
1967	38.2
1968	38.5
1969	37.6
1970	36.8

Source: *Current Population Reports, P-60 Series.*

for these families are lower than those for other families. Answering that question will involve us in matters similar to those discussed in the previous chapter. However, before we attack that problem, it will be useful to consider a second aspect of the female-all family poverty

Table 2

RELATIVE INCOME OF FAMILIES WITH A FEMALE HEAD, UNITED STATES, 1947-70

Year	Relative Income*
1947	0.70
1948	0.63
1949	0.66
1950	0.56
1951	0.58
1952	0.55
1953	0.56
1954	0.53
1955	0.54
1956	0.56
1957	0.54
1958	0.52
1959	0.49
1960	0.51
1961	0.50
1962	0.50
1963	0.49
1964	0.50
1965	0.49
1966	0.51
1967	0.52
1968	0.49
1969	0.48
1970	0.48

Source: *Current Population Reports,*
   P-60 Series.

* Ratio of median income of families with female head to median income of families with male head.

differential, *viz.*, the tendency in the post-World War II era for the ratio of the poverty rate for female families to that for all families to increase (again, see Table 1). We have already referred to this in passing, for it is implied by the lack of decline in the female poverty rate between 1947 and 1959 and the relatively slow rate of decrease in that rate since then.

It is quite easy to understand why the poverty rate for families headed by a woman failed to decline in the early post-World War II period. In those years, there was a marked deterioration in the relative income position of such families. Observe the data of Table 2. There, we show the ratio of the median income of families with a female head to the median income of families with a male head. In 1947, that ratio was .70 and by 1959, it had fallen to .49. This is a tremendous change; one certainly capable of explaining the failure of the female family poverty rate to decrease in this period.

Beyond 1959, however, the relative income position of female families does not continue to deteriorate. Rather, it stabilizes at about 50 percent of the income level of families headed by a male. This being the case, a reasonable expectation would be that economic growth would have a similar impact on the poverty rates for both male and female headed families. Obviously, this has not occurred. To understand why, we must explore in some depth the sources of income for families headed by a woman. From various data sources, we can determine that only about 60 percent of female heads of families are engaged in work activity (see Table 3). And, of those 60 percent, only about one-half are

Table 3

1970 LABOR MARKET STATUS,
FEMALE HEADS OF HOUSEHOLD

Status	Number (000's)	Percent
Working Full Time	2171	36.5
Year Round	1894	31.8
Less than Year Round	277	4.7
Working Part Time	1446	24.3
Not Working	2333	39.2
Total	5950	100.0

Source: *Current Population Reports, P-60 Series.*

engaged in full time, year round work activity. Thus, in total, slightly less than one-third of female heads of families work full time throughout the year. Contrast this with the 68.7 percent of male heads of families who work full time year round.

The relatively small emphasis on full time work activity among female family heads would seem to require some explanation. Two possibilities readily come to mind. First, given the relatively low level of earnings received by women,[1] it might well be that, compared to non-work activity, work is less attractive for women, particularly when alternative sources of income in the form of transfer payments (such as general assistance, aid for dependent children, and the like) are readily available. In short, women may well simply choose not to work full time due to the fact that the earnings they would receive from working are not sufficiently larger than the income they will receive if they do not work to compensate them for the effort of working. This can be thought of as a voluntary decision not to work full time.

The second possible explanation for the relative lack of full time work activity among female family heads is that they really want to work full time, but are either unable to do so (1) because of health problems or (2) cannot find a job. These can be viewed as involuntary reasons for not working full time.

Making a distinction between voluntary and involuntary reasons for female heads of family not working full time is of more than casual significance. The public policy implications of these alternatives are quite different. If women do not work full time due to illness or a lack of job opportunities, the transfer payment income they receive is probably regarded by them as inferior to the earnings produced by full time work. This follows from the fact that they seemingly would prefer the work income to the non-work income. On the other hand, if women choose not to work for essentially voluntary reasons, the combination of non-work income and leisure (i.e., not working) would seem to be preferable in their minds to full time work and its associated earnings. In this latter case, it can be argued that making transfer payment income available, largely through the so-called "welfare" system, to female heads of families has led to an increase in their social welfare.[2] By contrast, when, for involuntary reasons, they do not work full time, the transfer payment income they receive represents an inferior social welfare position compared to what they would have if they were able to work full time.

The question now is which of these explanations provides the better description of the behavior of women who are heads of families. Fortunately, we do have some information with respect to the reasons female family heads give for either not working or only working part time. These are summarized in Table 4 for the year 1970. Of the reasons listed there, two clearly belong in the involuntary category, illness or disability and inability to find work. The others represent essentially voluntary decisions, resulting from a desire to "keep house," attend school, or "other" reasons which are mostly of the "retirement" variety. On the basis of this classification, it appears that the dominant reasons for female heads of families not working full time are the voluntary ones. Among those who do not work at all, 77.1 percent gave reasons of the voluntary type. The pattern is not as pronounced with those who work part time. Only 60.8 percent of these women worked part time "voluntarily." Even so, the voluntary reasons for not working full time apparently are substantially more important than the involuntary.[3]

A few simple calculations are sufficient to provide us with some additional insight into the significance of the distinction between

Table 4

REASONS FOR NOT WORKING OR
WORKING PART TIME, FEMALE HEADS
OF HOUSEHOLD, 1970

Reason	Not Working		Working Part Time	
	Number (000's)	Percent	Number (000's)	Percent
Looking for Work or Could Not Find Work	45	1.9	349	24.1
Illness or Disability	489	21.0	218	15.1
Keeping House	1573	67.4	731	50.6
Attending School	33	1.4	55	3.8
Other*	194	8.3	93	6.4
Total	2333**	100.0	1446	100.0

Source: *Current Population Reports, P-60 Series.*

* Mostly retirement.

** Total does not equal sum of parts due to rounding.

voluntary and involuntary reasons for not working full time. In Table 5, estimates of the number of families with a female head that can be considered as being below the poverty line are provided for those who worked full time and for those who did not work full time according to whether they had voluntary or involuntary reasons for not working full time. The data shown there indicate that in over 60 percent of the cases where a family with a female head is classified as being in poverty, the head was not working full time for voluntary reasons. Be careful, though, in interpreting this statistic. It does not mean that these families are "voluntarily" living in poverty. What it does suggest, however, is that provision of additional full time work opportunities of the kind presently available to women would probably have a small impact on the incidence of poverty among families with a female head.

Table 5

LABOR FORCE STATUS AND REASONS
FOR NOT WORKING FULL TIME,
FEMALE HEADS OF FAMILIES WITH
POVERTY LEVELS OF INCOME,
UNITED STATES, 1970

Status	Number (000's)	Percent
Working Full Time	302	13.8
Working Part Time	668	30.5
Voluntarily	448	20.5
Involuntarily	220	10.0
Not Working	1220	55.7
Voluntarily	900	41.1
Involuntarily	320	14.6
Total Not Working Full Time	1888	86.2
Voluntarily	1348	61.6
Involuntarily	540	24.6
Total	2190	100.0

Source: *Current Population Reports, P-60 Series.*

This follows from the evidence that the substantial majority of the heads of these families are already behaving in a fashion that implies disinterest in such opportunities.[4]

The evidence to this point leads toward the conclusion that there is much greater reliance on non-work income among families with a female head than in the society as a whole. This is confirmed by other data which indicate that about one-half (45.4 percent) of females who received income in 1970 had income from sources other than earnings, and one-fourth (25.4 percent) had only income of this type.Details are provided in Table 6. The significance of this is magnified by the specific nature of the "other" income received by women. Compared to male recipients of income, almost twice as many women (in percentage

Table 6

SOURCES OF INCOME, FEMALES, UNITED STATES, 1970

Type of Income	Percent Receiving
Earnings	54.5
Wages and Salaries only	51.9
Self Employment only	2.1
Wages and Salaries and Self Employment	0.5
Earnings and Other Income	20.0
Wages and Salaries and Other	18.3
Self Employment and other	1.3
Wages and Salaries, Self Employment, and Other	0.4
Other Income only	25.4

Source: *Current Population Reports, P-60 Series.*

Table 7

SOURCES OF OTHER INCOME,
BY SEX, UNITED STATES, 1970

Type of Income	Percent Receiving*	
	Male	Female
Social Security and Railroad Retirement	26.6	46.9
Dividends, Interest, Rents, etc.	67.9	46.4
Public Assistance and Welfare	4.6	14.6
Unemployment Compensation, Workmen's Compensation, and Government Pensions	24.0	15.3
Private Pensions, Annuities, and Alimony	10.1	14.5

Source: *Current Population Reports, P-60 Series.*

* Since one individual may receive more than one type of income, percentages do not add to 100.0.

terms) were receiving social security or railroad retirement benefits, almost three times as many were recipients of public assistance and/or welfare, and about one and one-half times as many were beneficiaries of private pensions, annuities, or alimony (See Table 7). In the other direction, a larger proportion of men were receiving dividends, interest, or rents as well as unemployment compensation, workmen's compensation, and government pensions. Clearly, the mix of the "other" income received by women is much more heavily in the direction of pure transfer payment income, particularly of the "welfare" type.

But, what does this all mean from the standpoint of the problem of why poverty rates among families with a female head have been less sensitive to increases in the overall level of economic activity in the economy than the poverty rate in general? A great deal: For example, almost three and one-half million women were receiving public assistance and welfare type income in 1970. A substantial portion of these are heads of families and many of these families have levels of income that place them in the poverty category. The heavy dependence on income of this type among the female families characterized by poverty means that their income levels are not as responsive to changes in economic activity since those changes are reflected primarily in levels of work related earnings. Further, if levels of transfer payment income are increased, there may be a tendency to further mute the effects of changes in levels of work related income. This occurs because increases in transfer income make it relatively more attractive compared to work related income, particularly for those women who would receive full time work income below the average for such activity. In that case, they might simply prefer transfer (i.e., "welfare") income to work income and if they make such a choice, the apparent effect of increases in general levels of income on poverty rates among families with a female head will be less than expected. Interestingly, there is evidence that this kind of substitution did occur during the decade of the 1960's. First, in 1959, only 37.8 percent of women received other earnings compared to the 45.4 percent in 1970. Also, in 1959, median income for all female families was 49.6 percent as great as median income for female families whose head worked full time. By 1970, that percentage had *increased* to 56.8. This is consistent with the premise that female family heads substituted other types of income for earnings from full time work during the 1960's.

II. SOURCES OF DIFFERENTIAL EARNINGS FOR WOMEN

While our conclusions to now have been useful, they have skirted to a certain extent the critical issue that is involved in the question of the economic status of women in the United States, namely, the causes of the substantial differential between income levels for women and men. The importance of that differential cannot be overemphasized. For example, even though we concluded that much of the lack of responsiveness of the female family poverty rate stemmed from a "voluntary" substitution of transfer payment income for full time work related earnings, we said nothing about the fact that the relative attractiveness of the transfer payment income is largely the result of the low levels of earnings of women. If the average earnings of women more closely approached those of men, the available transfer payment income would not be nearly as alluring to women who are heads of household.

To be consistent with our earlier discussions, we should approach the question of the male-female earnings differential using the same general framework for analysis. Two basic explanations of earnings differences have been suggested: (1) variations in the quantity of genetic human capital possessed by individuals and (2) "discrimination" against certain groups of people, either through denying them access to acquired human capital or in the form of employers paying two equally qualified and productive people different wages because of their belonging to a particular sub-group of the population. Again, the conventional hypothesis with respect to the male-female earnings differential is that "discrimination" is the source of the problem. However, in this case there is a somewhat narrower focus with the emphasis being much more on employer behavior than on the denial of access to acquired human capital. The available evidence clearly indicates that the levels of formal education of men and women are almost identical, although it can be argued that this is not the case at the extremely advanced levels of professional training (post-baccalaureate).[5] But, as a general proposition, it is difficult to explain the pervasiveness of male-female earnings differentials on the basis of differences in the level of formal education of males and females. Thus, as a broad-gauge explanation of disparities in earnings by sex, patterns of formal education seem to offer very little.

I suspect that a slight digression is in order at this point. To a dedicated member of the "women's liberation" movement, it must seem that I have overlooked the obvious, the content of the formal education that is provided in our society. It has become almost an article of faith within the "movement" to decry the insidious "sexist" bias that permeates educational materials and leads to women being "indoctrinated" with notions of their being inferior, etc. Hardly a month passes that one does not find in his (or her) daily newspaper a description of some new study detailing this type of bias. For example, recently a researcher "discovered" that the depictions of the economic role of men and women in elementary school text books is "biased" in the direction of creating stereotypes of women's economic activity by showing them as being predominantly teachers, nurses or housewives. On the other hand, men are depicted in a much wider variety of jobs. Interesting, and perhaps indicative of some types of bias (either intentional or unintentional) on the part of the males who write such books. Wait, though! The books are largely written by women. And, the elementary education system is largely dominated by women. How does this square with the hypothesis of "sexist" bias? Very neatly, in the minds of those dedicated to the "movement." Clearly, the fact that female authors depict women in this stereotyped fashion is indicative of how thoroughly the male dominated society structures the minds of women. In short, these authors are simply the feminine equivalent of "Uncle Toms," i.e., "traitors" to their sex.

All this is a very convenient type of reasoning. Essentially, what it means is that if the "movement" finds something it objects to and it originates with males, it is "sexist" in character. On the other hand, if it originates with females, it is also "sexist" in nature because women have been, so to speak, "tricked" into doing it. That way, the "sexist" hypothesis can never be refuted and the members of the "movement" can establish themselves as the guardians of women's rights (as defined by them). Of course, what this means is that the "movement" has become religious in character with its own set of "high priestesses" (the

Gloria Steinem's, etc.). That kind of logic really offers little in the way of satisfactory intellectual explanations for the male-female earnings differential. To illustrate its sterility, take the elementary textbook example. An alternative hypothesis is that the authors of these textbooks are depicting the world approximately as it is. We may object to that reality, but is it really the function of textbooks to depict the world as it should be or as some group thinks it ought to be? Perhaps, but this is not the place to argue that question. The point is that the "movement" logic is incapable of dealing with this alternative.

While there is little difference in the quantity of formal education received by males and females, this is not the only form of acquired human capital. In addition, there is training received in the context of one's job situation, i.e., on-the-job training. Here, it is not at all clear that males and females are treated in a similar fashion. Viewed from the standpoint of an employer, the expected return to him from on the job training of a worker is dependent on the expected length of his (or her) employment. The longer an employee is expected to remain in a particular employment, the more potentially remunerative it is for an employer to provide him (or her) with on-the-job training. The available evidence rather strongly suggests that the labor force status of women is more susceptible to change than that of men.[6] There are logical reasons for this. The employment tenure of women is more likely to be interrupted than that of men for at least two reasons: (1) marriage and child rearing and (2) job changing by a husband that moves a wife to a different geographic area.

One point is worth noting here. While the generalizations employers make about the permanence of a woman's attachment to her employment may be entirely valid, in individual cases, they may be quite inaccurate. Of course, this is true of any generalization. It represents a perception of average or typical behavior. Since the on-the-job-training decision involves a prediction of the future actions of an employee, some basis for forecasting behavior is needed and typical past patterns of employment activity may be as good a guide as any. Nevertheless, women who stay in their jobs unusually long periods of time may be denied equal access with men to on-the-job-training. All this means is that their prospects for job advancement may be hindered, simply because they are females and employer's actions toward females are predicated on their typical or average behavior.

For now, we will ignore the general question of "pure" employer discrimination against women, i.e., the payment of lower wages to women on some basis other than their differential human capital endowment, and turn to the matter of possible differences between males and females in the quantity and type of genetic human capital they possess. In this respect, we can dispense with the major source of genetic human capital differentials that dominated the discussion of Chapter Six, namely, differences in mental ability as measured by standard tests. There is absolutely no evidence of any difference between men and women in their average level of mental ability. There may be some indications of differential patterns of ability.[7] However, all this would suggest is that men would have a comparative advantage in certain areas and women in others. Given the consistency across broad occupational categories of earnings differentials unfavorable to women (see Table 8), it would not seem appropriate to attach much significance to this. Therefore, it does not seem appropriate to hypothesize any important differences in the level of mental genetic human capital by sex.

An absence of differences by sex in endowment with mental human capital of the genetic type has one very interesting implication. An examination of the full set of data presented in Table 8 shows that the occupational distribution of women is more heavily weighted with the low income occupations than is the male distribution. Specifically, 57.2 percent of males in non-agricultural occupations are employed in the four highest paid activities, while only 30.3 percent of women are in those types of employment. If we accept the idea that there is some significant relationship between earnings levels and mental ability, the difference between the male and female occupational mix suggests that,

Table 8

OCCUPATIONAL DISTRIBUTION AND MEDIAN INCOME
LEVELS, BY OCCUPATION, BY SEX, NON-AGRICULTURAL
EMPLOYMENT, UNITED STATES, 1970

Occupation	Percent Distribution		Median Income	
	Male	Female	Male	Female
Professional, Technical and Kindred	14.6	16.3	$11,577	$6,675
Managers, Officials, and Proprietors	15.7	5.2	11,292	5,523
Clerical	7.0	35.9	7,965	4,646
Sales	6.7	7.5	8,321	2,279
Craftsmen and Kindred	20.2	1.3	8,833	4,276
Operatives and Kindred	19.3	14.0	7,017	3,885
Service	8.9	18.8	5,568	2,541
Laborers	7.6	1.0	4,839	3,151

Source: *Current Population Reports, P-60 Series.*

from the mental standpoint, women may be consistently over-qualified for the jobs they hold. A similar line of reasoning would also suggest the approximate equality of male and female possession of acquired human capital of the formal education variety likely means that typically women possess more human capital of this type than is required for the jobs they perform. This redundancy of various forms of human capital might explain some of the observed male-female earnings differential, for women may be able to capture only the economic rewards appropriate to the average level of such human capital in their particular occupations.[8]

Mental genetic human capital is not the only consideration, though. In our earlier chapters, we employed examples of genetic human capital that were of a physical nature. The possibility of differential physical endowments that might affect economic performance is particularly important from the standpoint of the male-female earnings differential. Even the most ardent supporter of women's rights will find it difficult to argue that there are no physiological differences between men and women. The question is not whether such differences exist, but whether they have an adverse effect on the productive capacity of women. In certain types of employment, it would seem that these differences would be important. Consider occupational callings that require very great amounts of pure physical strength. On the average, women could not perform these tasks as well as men. Therefore, there would either be exclusion of women from these types of employment or, in the absence of exclusion, women would probably be paid less than men for this work.

As a generalized explanation for lower female earnings, differences in physical genetic human capital are not especially attractive. In some types of employment, yes, but, in such occupations as the professional and managerial areas? Much more doubtful. However, as a partial explanation of the male-female earnings differential, the physical human capital disparity may be quite feasible.

This leaves only the "pure" discrimination explanation for lower female earnings. In effect, this is a residual factor, i.e., whatever we can't explain by other influences is an indication of "pure" discrimination. But, why would such discrimination exist? A variety of answers are possible. It just may be that many employers simply automatically regard women as not being as capable as men. This is a viable hypothesis. But, how can we determine whether this is the case? For that matter, how can we evaluate the validity of the various alternative hypotheses that have been discussed? There is no easy answer to that question. In fact, only a limited amount of data that can truly be considered to yield reasonably authoritative conclusions is available. Specifically, the data referred to in Chapter Six for the manufacturing sector of the economy are useful here. These data permit us to estimate the impact of female employment on wages and productivity levels in manufacturing industries. Remember, in this analysis, differences in the quantity of educational human capital possessed by workers and the amount of physical capital employed in the particular productive process are held constant statistically.

The procedure for testing for the presence of pure discrimination distinguishes between situations where there is or is not exclusion of females from employment. In the case of no exclusion of women, the analysis reveals that both wage rates and average productivity levels are significantly related in a negative fashion to the level of female employment. This substantiates the hypothesis that productivity levels are negatively affected by hiring women employees. However, in contrast to the white-non-white case, the difference in wage levels is not that which would be expected on the basis of the productivity differential. In fact, it is larger than what it should be. This rather strongly indicates the presence of pure discrimination against women in manufacturing employment.

This finding is confirmed when those instances where females are relatively excluded from employment are considered. Here, the findings are that there is no relationship between average productivity and the level of female employment. This is quite consistent with the existence of systematically lower productivity by females working in the manufacturing sector. Such a differential would explain the exclusion of women from employment. The truly revealing aspect of this analysis is the relationship between wage and female employment levels. The greater the level of female employment, the lower the wage level, despite the absence of productivity differentials. Also, the wage differential associated with female employment is almost exactly equal to the excess of the wage over the productivity differential that is observed in the no exclusion case. Again, the clear implication is that there is some type of "pure" discrimination against females in at least some labor markets.

While the evidence we have presented is limited in scope and character, it does suggest that the explanation of the observed differential between male and female earnings is a multiple one, including elements of "pure" discrimination, differential endowment of genetic human capital of the physical type, and, possibly, less acquired human capital of the on-the-job-training variety. Such a multi-faceted approach to explaining these differentials is not conducive to simplistic generalizations. Rather, we must be content with some degree of indeterminacy while recognizing that part of the observed differential is the product of factors that reduce the productivity levels of women, while part stems from an apparent willingness on the part of employers to discriminate against women.

III. CONCLUSIONS

What can we broadly conclude about the sources of poverty among women in the United States, particularly those who are heads of households? First, given the earnings potential of women in the labor market and the levels of transfer payment income available to them through such sources as public assistance and welfare payments, a very substantial portion of female heads of household apparently elect not to work full time and to substitute the transfer income for full time work related earnings. Further, it does appear that there has been a tendency for this substitution to increase over the past decade. The end result is that the poverty rate among these families is quite a bit less sensitive to increases in the general level of income in the economy. This has produced the phenomenon of a substantial *relative* increase in the amount of poverty found among families with a female head. In short, a case can be made for the applicability of the "backwash" thesis where families headed by a woman are concerned.

On the basis of these findings, it appears that a major contributing factor to the relative increase in poverty among families headed by a female is the comparatively low levels of full time work related earnings received by women. It is this, more than anything else, which probably pushes more female heads of families away from full time work activity and into the so-called "welfare" system. Of course, in one respect this may not be a total loss for the society. It may well be in the social interest to reduce the number of female heads of household who are working full time, due to the impact such work activity has on the fabric of the involved families. However, that is a judgmental question that lies outside the scope of this volume. Nevertheless, this possibility should be recognized.

Finally, the ultimate source of the deviant behavior of the poverty rate for families headed by a female appears to be a combination of environmental factors (discriminatory attitudes on the part of employers) and physiological differences between men and women. Clearly, to the extent that environmental factors are involved, the relative poverty status of the female family may be improved by such public policy approaches as equal opportunity legislation and the like. However, it would seem to be quite unlikely that this approach will lead to a full solution to this problem.

FOOTNOTES

[1]The male-female earnings differential is almost universally unfavorable to women. Detailed data by occupation are presented later in the chapter.

[2]The argument here is simple. The combination of leisure and income that people choose for themselves reflects what they think is best for them, given the constraints they face. Thus, if making transfer

payment income available to female heads of household causes them to voluntarily alter their patterns of work activity, it would seem that they would be moving to a leisure-income combination that is preferable to their previous one. Therefore, altering the constraints facing these women by making transfer income available to them has had the effect of improving their social welfare position.

[3]One must be careful with data of this type since they involve people stating what they think is the reason for their behavior. They may unconsciously distort the reasons they give. For example, a person says he is "too sick to work." That may well be true, but only because he has transfer payment type income available to him (or her). In the absence of such income, that individual might well disregard his illness and work anyways in order to provide some minimal level of income. In general, my impression is that the more likely biases in data of this sort are in the direction of overstating the incidence of involuntary reasons for not working full time. Therefore, given the strong tendency toward showing voluntary reasons for not working full time, we will use this information here.

[4]On the other hand, among poverty families headed by a male, only 37.8 percent of those heads not working full time indicated voluntary reasons for their labor force status. Source: *Current Population Reports, P-60 Series.*

[5]For example, as of the 1970 Census, 13.1 percent of males aged 25 years of age or over had four or more years of college education, while only 8.1 percent of females 25 years of age or over had training at that level. Source: United States Census, *General Social and Economic Characteristics, United States Summary*, United States Department of Commerce, Bureau of the Census, Washington, D.C., 1972, Table 75.

[6]For evidence on this matter, see the classic study by Bowen, William G., and Finegan, T. Aldrich, *The Economics of Labor Force Participation.* Princeton University Press: Princeton, New Jersey, 1969.

[7]For a summary of the literature related to these differences, see Lesser, et. al., *Mental Abilities of Children . . , op. cit.*, particularly, pp. 9-10.

[8]For example, a woman with Ph.D. training functioning as a secretary (not an executive secretary, though) would undoubtedly not capture the economic rent normally accorded to Ph.D. trained individuals.

[9]The rationale for such exclusion is provided in Chapter Six.

CHAPTER 8

THE AGED AND POVERTY

Any reasonably complete treatment of poverty in America must deal with the subject of poverty among the aged. Defined in terms of the basic standard employed throughout this volume, poverty among families with an aged head is substantially greater than it is in the society as a whole (see Table 1).[1] In addition, the available data also indicate that in the post-World War II period, the poverty rate among aged families behaved in a fashion somewhat similar to that found among families with a female head, i.e., it tended to decline much less rapidly than the poverty rate in general. As a consequence, this period has been characterized by a *relative* increase in the amount of poverty among aged families. This would seem to suggest that the aged in America might be a prime example of the "backwash" thesis at work. But, let us withhold judgment on that point until later.

I. THE SOURCE OF THE RELATIVE INCREASE IN AGED POVERTY

The relative increase in poverty among aged families comes as something of a disappointment, largely because the post-World War II era has been characterized by a tremendous increase in the volume of transfer payment income directly available to the aged. In 1945, old age benefits under the Social Security system[2] plus old age assistance payments totaled about six-tenths of one percent of personal income in the United States (see Table 2). Currently, these sources of income for the aged amount to almost five percent of personal income. This represents about an eight-fold increase in the relative amount of the nation's income being devoted to maintaining income levels among the aged. Of course, part of this increase is due to a steady growth in the percentage of the country's population that belongs in the aged category. However, adjusting for this still leaves over a six-fold increase in the relative amount of this type transfer payment income.[3]

The puzzling (at least at first) aspect of this sizable increase in the amount of transfer payment income provided to the aged is its apparent negative impact on the relative income position of the aged. Table 1 also provides information on the ratio of the median income of aged families to the median income of all families in the United States. That ratio has obviously declined in the post-World War II period. As of 1947, it was about 0.60 while it is now approximately 0.50.

Table 1

RELATIVE INCOME OF FAMILIES WITH
AN AGED HEAD AND PERCENT OF SUCH
FAMILIES WITH INCOME LESS THAN $3,000
IN 1963 PRICES, UNITED STATES, 1947-70

Year	Relative Income*	Percent with Income Less than $3,000
1947	0.60	51.3
1950	0.58	55.0
1956	0.53	50.7
1957	0.50	53.5
1958	0.52	52.3
1959	0.52	50.0
1960	0.52	49.8
1961	0.53	48.5
1962	0.54	46.5
1963	0.55	44.9
1964	0.51	44.1
1965	0.50	44.0
1966	0.49	42.4
1967	0.49	41.0
1968	0.53	35.8
1969	0.51	35.9
1970	0.51	35.3

Source: *Current Population Reports, P-60 Series.*

*Ratio of median income of families with an aged head to median income of all families.

However, just as in the case of the female family, the bulk of the decline took place in the 1950's.

So much for the facts of the situation. The question now is, "Why?" Actually, there is a fairly straightforward reason for the deterioration in the relative income position of aged families in the face of a great increase in their access to transfer payment income. At the beginning of the post-World War II period, almost one-half of all men aged 65 and over were members of the labor force, i.e., they were either employed or actively seeking work. By contrast, currently only a little more than 25 percent of aged males are in that category. This substantial shift of

Table 2

OLD AGE BENEFITS UNDER SOCIAL SECURITY
AND OLD AGE ASSISTANCE AS PERCENTAGE
OF PERSONAL INCOME, UNITED STATES,
1944-45 to 1967-68

Fiscal Year	Personal Income (billions)	Old Age Benefits plus Old Age Assistance	
		Amount (billions)	As % of Personal Income
1944-1945	171.1	1.0	0.58
1949-1950	227.6	2.3	1.01
1954-1955	310.9	6.1	1.96
1959-1960	401.0	13.0	3.24
1964-1965	538.9	18.6	3.45
1967-1968	628.8	30.4	4.83

Source: *Social Security Bulletin,* various years.

aged men away from labor force activity has resulted in a substitution of transfer payment income for wage income among this group.[4] This is the same type of shift that was observed among female heads of household in Chapter Seven.

The significance of the shift from work related to transfer payment income again turns on whether the change has been essentially a "voluntary" or an "involuntary" one. Let me emphasize again that the difference between "voluntary" and "involuntary" changes in labor market status is more than mere semantics. Involuntary changes suggest that the availability of work opportunity for the aged has been progressively declining in the post-World War II era. On the other hand, voluntary shifts imply that the aged have been systematically reducing their labor force activity in response to the increased availability of transfer payment income to the aged.. While the effect of both of these explanations of the shift in labor force patterns is essentially the same—the aged have less work related income and, consequently, their money income position relative to the rest of the economy deteriorates—their implications for the social welfare of the aged are quite different. In a free society, it is one thing to be denied work related income because of a lack of job opportunity and quite something else to relinquish work related income in exchange for increased leisure, for this is essentially what is involved in the "voluntary" decision to reduce work activity.

From the public policy side of things, the difference between voluntary and involuntary reduction of labor force participation by the aged is also critically important. One of the major elements of the broad complex of social programs that have been developed in the United States over the past 40 years is the Social Security system. It has many dimensions, but its primary one is the provision of income to the aged as a matter of right rather than as a matter of need.[5] Whether that phase of its operation can be judged successful depends on the voluntary-involuntary distinction. To understand why this is so, it is necessary that we explore the implications of this distinction in more depth.

To begin, we must define somewhat more carefully the objective of a program such as the Social Security system. Its goal is to do more than simply provide money income for the aged. Money income itself is presumably a vehicle through which the aged can improve their general level of well-being, i.e., their welfare. Whether the present system achieves that end depends crucially on whether the aged's reduction of their work activity is voluntary or involuntary. If the observed decline in labor force activity is involuntary in character, our attempts at providing income for the aged have not increased their well-being over what it would have been had they continued to work as they had in the past, for, presumably, an involuntary change in work patterns of the aged that results in a relative reduction of their levels of income does not enhance their happiness. In fact, if this is the case, it could be argued that all that has been accomplished by the sizable increase in the quantity of transfer payment income made available to the aged is staving off utter economic deprivation. In short, if this is true, our massive social insurance system has acted as nothing more than a less than perfect substitute for other forms of welfare payments. This would imply that the apparent relative impoverishment of the aged suggested by the money income statistics also indicates a worsening of their social welfare position.

On the other hand, if the changes in work habits are voluntary in character, the individuals who have made these decisions presumably feel that their welfare is enhanced by their "new" behavioral pattern. Thus, if they elect one combination of income and leisure over another, they reveal a preference for that combination and indicate that they are happier or more satisfied with it. In this instance, the fact that they elect a lower level of income does not indicate a decline in their welfare—quite the contrary; it would seem to indicate an improvement in welfare. In effect, it can be argued that under these conditions, the Social Security system has operated to provide the elderly with an additional degree of freedom—freedom to alter their basic living pattern to include greater quantities of leisure than would otherwise be possible. Of course, such an alteration in the style of living of the aged leads to a reduction in money income in that leisure has no money price attached to it in our society and, therefore, its presence is not reflected in money income statistics. However, as already noted, the reduction in money income implicit in a voluntary increase in leisure among the elderly does not necessarily imply a deterioration in the social welfare position of the aged, but may be indicative of an improvement in it. This would suggest that the relative impoverishment of the aged in a money income sense would not mean impoverishment in a broad welfare sense.

Having established the importance of whether the reduction of work activity by the aged is voluntary or involuntary, the problem now is to determine which is the case. In the parlance of the economist, this comes down to deciding whether the observed changes in labor force behavior arise out of shifts in the demand for the labor services of the aged (which would reduce job opportunity) or from negative shifts in the supply of aged labor (due to their decision to voluntarily reduce their labor force activity).

The first of these possibilities can be formally analyzed with the assistance of the economic theory of discrimination.[6] That analysis suggests two possible end results of the relative demand for older workers being less than that for younger workers: either (1) unemployment among older workers or (2) a wage differential that is unfavorable to older workers.[7] In turn, this argues that if there has been a change between two points in time that has adversely affected the demand for older workers, this change will be accompanied by either (1) a worsening of unemployment among the aged relative to younger workers or (2) a worsening of the relative wage position of older workers. Unemployment rates for males aged 65 and over are presented in Table 3. When these are compared with the unemployment rates for males aged 25-34 (also shown in Table 3), it is clear that the relative unemployment position of aged males has not worsened in the post-World War II period.

Data describing wage rates by age are difficult to find. Perhaps the most useful information that is available describes median income levels of male full time, year round workers who are aged 65 and over. These data are available for most of the post-World War II period and show that the median income of aged males working full time, year round quite consistently has been about three-fourths as large as the median income of all male full time year round workers.[8] These data are also consistent with information collected by the Social Security Administration describing the earnings levels of male workers who worked all four quarters of the year. These also show no deterioration in the relative earnings position of aged males.

Clearly, the available income and unemployment data do not support the demand shift (i.e., involuntary) explanation for changes in the labor force behavior of the aged. However, rejection of the demand shift thesis does not automatically imply acceptance of the proposition that

Table 3

UNEMPLOYMENT RATES, MALES, AGE 25-34
AND AGE 65 AND OVER,
UNITED STATES, 1947-1971

Year	Unemployment Rate	
	Age 25-34	Age 65 and over
1947	3.4 %	2.8 %
1948	2.8	3.4
1949	5.2	5.1
1950	4.4	4.8
1951	2.3	3.5
1952	2.2	3.0
1953	2.2	2.4
1954	4.8	4.4
1955	3.3	4.0
1956	3.3	3.5
1957	3.3	3.4
1958	6.5	5.2
1959	4.7	4.8
1960	4.8	4.2
1961	5.7	5.5
1962	4.5	4.6
1963	4.5	4.5
1964	3.5	4.0
1965	3.0	3.5
1966	2.4	3.1
1967	2.1	2.8
1968	1.9	2.9
1969	1.9	2.2
1970	3.4	3.3
1971	4.4	3.4

Source: *Manpower Report of the President, 1972,* Table A-15.

the observed decline in labor force activity among the aged is the result of their electing to enjoy more leisure due to the availability of greater quantities of transfer payment income. Some positive evidence to support a relationship between the presence of transfer payment in-come and labor force patterns of the aged is required before it can be accepted. Data supporting the presence of such a relationship are available and they indicate that providing the aged with transfer payment income of the type generated by our Social Security system significantly reduces their labor force activity.[9] In short, there is empirical support for the belief that the elderly have voluntarily elected increased leisure at the expense of higher levels of work related income.

The evidence supporting the hypothesis of a voluntary change in the labor force behavior of the aged receives additional support from data similar to those referred to in Chapter Seven. They indicate the reasons given by aged workers for either not working or working part time (see Table 4). When these reasons are classified as being "voluntary" or "involuntary" in character, we find that 76.8 percent of those not working offered voluntary reasons for their inactivity and 72.6 percent indicated that they worked part time for essentially voluntary reasons. This information is strongly consistent with the "voluntary" change hypothesis. Therefore, it would seem that the weight of the evidence argues strongly in favor of accepting this explanation for the labor force activity of the aged.

II. THE ADEQUACY OF LIVING STANDARDS AMONG THE AGED

The significance of the "voluntary" explanation for aged labor force behavior has already been discussed. However, it deserves re-emphasis.

Table 4

REASONS FOR AGED HEADS OF FAMILY NOT WORKING FULL TIME, UNITED STATES, 1970

Reason	Not Working		Working Part Time	
	Number (000's)	Percent	Number (000's)	Percent
Ill or Disabled	1030	22.6	208	18.4
Keeping House	456	10.0	52	4.6
Attending School	0	0.0	17	1.5
Could Not Find Work or Looking for Work	18	0.4	101	9.0
Other*	3059	67.0	751	66.5
Total	4563	100.0	1129	100.0

Source: *Current Population Reports, P-60 Series.*

* Mostly retirement.

Its major implication is that the relative deterioration in the income position of the aged (with its associated relative increase in measured poverty) is not indicative of a worsening of the social welfare position of the aged. Quite the contrary: It suggests the possibility that the system of income maintenance for the aged that has been developed through the Social Security system has led to an improvement in the level of social welfare of this group. But, how can this be? Doesn't the conventional wisdom in this respect argue that the relative economic condition of the aged has declined so rapidly that a true "crisis" is at hand? For example, consider the following quote from a Task Force document prepared for a series of hearings before the Special Committee on Aging of the United States Senate:[10]

> If old age is to be more than a period when people decline and die, some way must be found whereby the aged, who have helped in the past to provide the basis for rising living standards, are guaranteed a share in some of the "harvested fruits." What this requires is a substantial transfer of income from the working to the retired population in order to improve the *relative* economic status of the aged.[11]

Or:

> Even the level of living set by the Bureau of Labor Statistics /BLS/ in its Retired Couple's Budget is well beyond the means of most older people, especially for those who retired years ago. The average social security benefit of a couple retiring in 1950 met half the BLS budget cost then, but today /for the same couple/ it meets less than one-third.

These statements are reasonably representative of the Task Force report, a report that (1) is perhaps the best statement of what I have called the conventional wisdom in this area and (2) paints a picture of a precipitous decline in the relative economic status of the aged in America. Unfortunately, the logic of the report is suspect on several counts. As a case in point, much is made of the decline in the ratio of the average social security benefit of a retired couple to the BLS's Retired Couple's Budget for a Moderate Living Standard (hereafter referred to as the MLS budget). Given the importance of Social Security type income for the aged, this would seem to be imposing evidence of a relative decline in the economic status of the aged. However, it is somewhat misleading. The major difficulty with the conclusion advanced by the Task Force is that the MLS budget has risen over time much more rapidly than would be expected on the basis of increases in the general standard of living or increases in prices. Between December 1950 and December 1966, the MLS budget increased by 131 percent. During the same interval, wage levels in the economy rose by only 76 percent. If the MLS budget had increased by the same proportion as wage levels, it would have been only about three-fourths the figure the BLS reports. This would seem to indicate that changes in the MLS budget have been much more substantial than general advances in income over this period. However, these data overstate the relative increase in the *real* value of the MLS budget since prices for the commodities purchased by the aged appear to have increased more rapidly than prices in general. Specifically, the Bureau of Labor Statistics indicates that about one-half of the increase in the MLS budget between 1950 and 1966 was due to price increases. This means that prices for the market basket of commodities purchased by the aged rose by about 50 percent, whereas general price levels rose by only about 35 percent.

After adjustment for these differential price level changes, it can be estimated that the real increase in standard of living implied in the MLS budgets is in excess of 50 percent. By contrast, the change in real wage levels over the same period was only about 30 percent. Thus, the MLS budgets include increases in the real standard of living of the aged which are two-thirds greater than those enjoyed by the population as a whole. But, how can this be? Why has the MLS budget risen so much more rapidly in real terms than wage levels? The answer lies in the definition of the MLS budget. It is "intended to represent a measure of what *retired couples themselves consider an appropriate level of living.*"[12] I have deliberately emphasized a part of the quote that has been cited to make clear that it is the aged's own conception of what is a moderate standard of living that is determining in constructing this budget. Apparently, their perceptions of what is moderate have been shifting more rapidly than real living standards in the economy as a whole.

This should not be surprising. I suspect that it is generally true that people's conceptions of what is a moderate standard of living are very substantially affected by the standard of living they are currently enjoying. If this is true, it may well be that the more rapid increase in the real standard of living that is incorporated in the MLS budgets reflects nothing more than an improvement in the general standard of living of the aged. There is some evidence that this is precisely what has happened. For example, if we focus on the September-December retiree in 1965, we find that his old age benefits under Social Security would purchase approximately one-half of the MLS budget for December 1966—almost exactly the situation faced by the 1950 retiree *despite the more rapid increase in the real standard of living between 1950 and 1966 implied in these budgets.*

The data describing the relationship between average Social Security benefits and the MLS budget for the 1965 September-December retiree illustrate quite aptly the fallacy contained in making comparisons of the type found in the quote from the Task Force report. Such comparisons focus on changes in the relative economic position of the aged over the course of the full period of retirement rather than appraising changes over time in the average economic status of the aged during the retirement portion of their life. The type of comparison that is made is valuable for purposes of gaining insight into the stability of the relative income position of the aged throughout their retirement. However, it sheds little light on changes in the relative economic position of retirees who enter retirement at different points in time. For this type comparison, information such as that detailed for the 1965 September-December retiree is required.

Interestingly, this interpretation of the MLS budget data yields a conclusion that is exactly the opposite of what is suggested by the Task Force report, namely, that, on the average, transfer payment income of the Social Security type has increased during the post-World War II period in a fashion that leads to a higher relative standard of living for the aged. In combination with our earlier conclusion that changes in levels of labor force activity among the aged have been essentially voluntary in character and, thus, have contributed to increasing the social welfare of the aged, we seem to have arrived at a fairly unambiguous finding that the overall welfare position of the aged has been improving relatively over the past quarter century. This is not necessarily to argue that present levels of income among the aged are "satisfactory," whatever that may mean. Making that type of determination is largely a value judgment and therefore is primarily a personal thing. However, we can say with a reasonable degree of assurance that there is little validity to the idea that the relative economic status of the aged has been deteriorating at a rapid rate.

III. THE EARLY RETIREMENT PHENOMENON

One other bit of evidence relating to the economic condition of the elderly is available. Approximately a decade ago, the basic Social Security legislation was altered to provide men with the option of "retiring" when they reached age 62 with appropriate actuarial reductions in their Social Security benefits. The thinking within the Social Security Administration at this time was that making this alternative available would prove useful to those who had become unemployed or unable to work before they had reached age 65 and become eligible to receive old age benefits under Social Security.[13] The clear intention was that this option would provide some type of income maintenance other than general welfare for those who had become involuntarily displaced from work activity in the immediate pre-retirement years. Part and parcel of this reasoning was a strong belief that very few people would voluntarily elect this option since the reduced level of benefits would not be sufficient for them to "live on." This was quite consistent with the general view within the Social Security Administration that very few people "voluntarily" elected to reduce their level of work activity because of the availability of Social Security benefits. However, as we have seen, that is a substantially inaccurate perception of elderly behavior.

Similarly, the expectation that a relatively few aged males would avail themselves of the early retirement option was mistaken. Rather, there has been a flood of "early" retirements, so much so that a frequent theme in the previously discussed Task Force document is concern about the "problems" that early retirement is creating from the standpoint of income maintenance for the elderly. What frightens those who espouse the conventional wisdom is the prospect of approximately one-half of all recipients of old age benefits under Social Security receiving actuarially reduced payments.[14] Their unhappiness with that prospect reflects their almost exclusive preoccupation with money levels of income for the aged. Throughout our discussion, we have attempted to focus on the broader concept of levels of social welfare among the aged, which may or may not be synonomous with their money income levels. When viewed from this perspective, it is not so obvious that early retirement is creating additional problems. A simpler interpretation is to say that what the elderly are doing is electing a different lifetime pattern of income and leisure, one that is presumably preferable to the alternative of working until age 65 and then retiring.

That seems simple enough, doesn't it? Surely, one could not object to people choosing a pattern of behavior that they feel is better for them. Not unless one really believes that, in general, the individuals involved cannot be trusted to make a decision of this magnitude. Frankly, that is how a good many bureaucrats (and academicians, too, for that matter) think. They view the elderly as being much like little children who need to be guided into the proper course of action. Never mind that they may think they know what is best for them. If they are wise, they will behave as the bureaucrat thinks they should. No wonder the bureaucrat or academician becomes disturbed when a program such as early retirement receives such widespread acceptance. All he typically sees is a reduction in money income levels for the aged, meanwhile missing the essence of the decision, which is the substitution of leisure for income. On the other hand, the economist's framework of thinking tends to emphasize this aspect of the behavior of the elderly, i.e., the process of making choices.

Why this difference in perspective with respect to the economic behavior of the aged? Essentially, it arises out of a different definition of the term "choice." To the economist, a choice is a decision between alternatives, whatever they may be. To non-economists, however, the term "choice" more frequently denotes electing one alternative from among a set of "desirable" possibilities where the definition of whether a choice is "desirable" rests with someone other than the decision maker himself. Thus, many people would argue that unless the elderly have a range of "desirable" choices, they really have no choice at all. An example of this thinking is the following quote:[15]

> We can . . . .define retirement for the poor as a poverty of choices. If the modern meaning of retirement is a range of choices in income and work opportunities, then by definition the poor cannot make a retirement decision. A narrow economic logic to the contrary can produce much mischief for public policy."

Unfortunately, this is not an atypical view. It permeates much thinking and frequently leads to some strange conclusions. For example, one line of argument goes as follows: (1) The elderly do not voluntarily leave the labor force (i.e., do not make a labor market choice) but are pushed out by unscrupulous employers who, realizing that Social Security benefits are available, abdicate their responsibilities to their employees and (2) the only cure for this situation is larger levels of Social Security benefits.[16] Now, if this argument is correct, it implies that the creation of the massive Social Security system has had the effect of shifting great numbers of the aged to a poorer position in terms of their welfare than they would enjoy if the system did not exist. In effect, it says that the Social Security system's presence actually reduces the degree of freedom of the aged by leading to their being denied labor market opportunities. If this really is the case, a good argument can be made for dismantling the entire system since it would seem that it may, in reality, have worsened the social welfare position of the aged. Certainly, it would call into serious question the second part of the argument which is that the system should be expanded. This is roughly akin to a physician prescribing medication for a patient and, upon finding that he merely becomes sicker, recommending that the dosage of the medicine be increased. I must admit that I prefer the interpretation we have put on the evidence, which, incidentally, is one that reflects quite favorably on the Social Security system as a device for improving the social welfare of the aged.

IV. CONCLUSIONS

One dominant theme has marked our discussion of the economic status of the aged. It is an optimistic one that maintains that despite the observed deterioration in the relative money income position of the aged over the past quarter century, their relative social welfare position has actually improved. This has been largely due to their voluntarily substituting leisure for work activity and transfer payments for work related income. Consequently, the apparent tendency of money income levels of the aged to be somewhat unresponsive to movements in the general level of income in the society does not mean that the aged can be thought of as being an example of the "backwash" thesis at work, at least in the sense that the "backwash" notion is employed to denote a group's becoming progressively more disadvantaged through time. Quite the contrary: Far from being a segment of the population that is being "left behind" by American society, the aged have actually improved their relative economic position over what it was at the beginning of the post-World War II period.

While it seems to be clear that the aged have been improving their economic status in the society, this does not mean that their relative level of income (and social welfare) is necessarily satisfactory. This point remains arguable and the analysis presented here does not provide a basis for answering that question. However, it does suggest that the aura of crisis that the conventional wisdom assigns to the matter of income maintenance for the aged is unwarranted. In particular, it would seem to be inappropriate to institute large scale changes in our present system of providing income for the aged due to some false sense of emergency.

FOOTNOTES

[1] This does not take into account poverty among unrelated individuals (i.e., individual people not living in family units). This is an important group among the aged. However, the general picture presented by the family poverty rates holds among this group.

[2] Old age benefits are what people usually regard as their "pension" from the Social Security system. They are strictly the retirement benefits that accrue to people as the result of their work activity during their lifetime.

[3] The proportion of the aged in the population increased from about eight percent to almost ten percent in the interval in question. For this reason alone, the proportion of personal income going to transfer payments for the aged would have risen by about 25 percent, even if payments to the average aged person (expressed as a fraction of per capita personal income) had remained unchanged.

[4] The magnitude of the change is accentuated by a decline in the intensity of labor force participation among the aged. There is now a greater tendency for part time work among the aged.

[5] Providing people with income as a matter of "right" simply means that they do not have to demonstrate a "need" for it as, for example, they must do in order to receive general assistance or welfare payments.

[6] For a discussion of the economics of discrimination, see Gary S. Becker, *The Economics of Discrimination, op. cit.*

[7] This evidence is presented in appendix B of my *The Retirement Decision: An Explanatory Essay, op. cit.*

[8]For example, in 1957, median earnings of full time, year round aged workers were 72.6 percent of those for all males who worked full time. In 1970, they were 73.5 percent of those for all full time male workers. Source: *Current Population Reports, P-60 Series.*

[9]*The Retirement Decision: An Exploratory Essay, op cit.*, Chapter V, and my "The Aged and the Extent of Poverty in the United States," *Southern Economic Journal*, October 1966, pp. 212-222.

[10]*Economics of Aging: Toward a Full Share in Abundance, Part I— Survey Hearings*, Hearings before Special Committee on Aging, United States Senate, Washington, D.C.: U.S. Government Printing Office, 1969, p. 158.

[11]*Ibid.*, p. 155.

[12]*Ibid.*, p. XIII.

[13]These remarks are based on my personal observations while employed at the Social Security Administration in the early 1960's.

[14]For details of the extent to which this has been happening, see *Manpower Economics, op. cit.*, p. 190.

[15]*Economics of Aging*, Part II, *op. cit.*, p. 292.

[16]I have stated this view in what some would regard as an extreme fashion. However, it seems to me that it does not unreasonably distort this particular position.

REGIONAL VARIATIONS IN POVERTY

There is one other major dimension of the poverty problem that needs to be considered—regional disparities in its incidence. These occur in three different forms that are significant. First, there is the general difference in income levels and poverty rates between the geographic area of the United States known as the "South" and the remainder of the country. Table 1 provides some detailed information on this point. Roughly, the median level of family income in the regions that comprise the South is about 80 to 85 percent of that found in the non-Southern parts of the country. Predictably, this leads to poverty rates in the South that are about 1.6 times as great as those found elsewhere. These differentials are clearly substantial and pose certain problems. For example, such lower income levels tend to give rise to differential regional per capita expenditures on education and varying amounts of transfer payment income of the welfare expenditure type. Differential

Table 1

FAMILY MEDIAN INCOME AND POVERTY RATES,
BY REGION, UNITED STATES,
1970

Region	Median Family Income	Poverty Rate*
Northeast	$10,696	10.1%
North Central	10,327	11.2
South	8,552	17.9
West	10,273	11.6

Source: *Current Population Reports, P-60 Series.*

* Defined as families with less than $3,000 in family income in 1963 prices.

regional levels of public expenditures on items such as these have serious implications in a society that is apparently dedicated to equality of educational opportunity and providing some general minimum level of income *irrespective of a person's living location.*

A second type of regional income differential is that which exists between the urban and rural portions of the United States. To a certain extent this duplicates the North-South differential since the Southern areas tend to be more rural than the non-Southern. However, the urban-rural income differential is a persistent one in all regions of the United States. This is clearly indicated by the data shown in Table 2. From these data, it can be seen that median incomes in urban areas are approximately one-third to one-half greater than those found in rural areas. This produces poverty rates in the rural areas that are about twice as great as those in the urban portion of the country. Income and poverty differentials of this magnitude create the same type of problems with respect to per capita levels of public expenditures that were noted in connection with the North-South income differential. However, to a certain extent, these problems may be more manageable since the urban-rural economic differentials are found within all state governmental jurisdictions which permits state by state actions to equalize per capita public expenditures in urban and rural areas within the states.

Table 2

FAMILY MEDIAN INCOME AND POVERTY RATES, BY LIVING LOCATION, UNITED STATES, 1970

Living Location	Median Family Income	Poverty Rate*
Farm	$ 6,733	27.1%
Non-Farm	10,006	12.3
Outside Metropolitan Area	8,348	17.8
Inside Metropolitan Area	10,789	10.1

Source: *Current Population Reports, P-60 Series.*

* Defined as families with less than $3,000 in family income in 1963 prices.

Finally, perhaps the most critical of the regional type income differentials is that which exists within large metropolitan areas between the inner city and suburban areas. These differentials have often produced some acrimonious disputes at the local level, largely, I suspect, because they are so obvious to the citizenry of metropolitan areas. For those living in the inner city portion of urban areas, the affluence of the suburban areas, particularly when it comes to such things as expenditures for public education, is frequently a source of friction between inner and outer city residents. This is understandable when the magnitude of the economic disparities is considered. Table 3 presents the pertinent data which indicate that the typical income level in the inner city portions of our large metropolitan areas is 20 percent less than that in the non-inner city areas. This produces poverty levels in the inner city that are about 70 percent greater than those in the suburbs.

Accentuating the problem of intra-metropolitan area economic differentials is the fact that they almost universally carry with them racial overtones. The racial mix of urban populations shows a markedly higher concentration of non-whites in the inner city than is found in the suburban areas.[1] The racial aspect of the intra-urban differentials seems to have more public impact than the other forms of regional wage differentials. This is probably due to the closer juxtaposition of population with differing racial mixes. In short, for those concerned,

Table 3

FAMILY MEDIAN INCOME LEVEL
AND POVERTY RATES, BY LIVING LOCATION
WITHIN METROPOLITAN AREAS,
UNITED STATES, 1970

Population of Metropolitan Area	Median Family Income		Poverty Rate*	
	Central City	Outside Central City	Central City	Outside Central City
1,000,000 or more	$9,900	$12,425	12.5 %	6.6 %
Less than 1,000,000	9,477	10,599	14.4	8.7

Source: *Current Population Reports, P-60 Series.*

* Defined as families with less than $3,000 in family income in 1963 prices.

the racial differences are "more obvious" than they are, for example, in the case of the North-South income differential. In the latter case, at least, there is also a North-South differential unfavorable to whites. While this is also true in the instance of intra-urban differentials, it seems to be largely overlooked. As a result, the stereotype of the non-white inner city and "lily-white" suburbs has developed. And, as is true with most stereotypes, it contains a substantial degree of inaccuracy.

The impact of the inner city-suburban income differential on expenditures for public services seems to present a much more critical problem than the other regional differentials. This is especially true in the educational area where one of the great controversies of recent years has turned on the disparity between the "quality" of suburban and inner city education. The fascinating thing is that the available evidence, especially the Coleman report,[3] suggests that educational "quality," as conventionally measured, bears little relationship to the level of expenditures for education. Nevertheless, within the inner cities, the insistence on greater outlays on education has been intense, frequently leading to a state of financial crisis. The saga of inner city education now consists primarily of a beleaguered school board attempting to react to a situation in which they are confronted by (1) pressures for improved educational "quality" (which all too often simply translates into greater expenditures for education), (2) increasingly militant demands by teachers (more and more frequently unionized) for higher salaries and better working conditions, and (3) a tax base that seriously restricts their capacity to meet the rising costs of education implied in the pressure for "quality" and the teachers' demands. And, at the heart of this problem are the forces that produce the intra-urban income differential. More will be said about this later.

I. THE SOURCES OF REGIONAL INCOME AND POVERTY DIFFERENTIALS

Granted that regional income and poverty differentials exist, the more interesting matter is why they occur. To answer that question, we will focus on the causes of the income differentials. If those can be explained, the reasons for the differences in poverty rates naturally follow. We will turn first to the North-South income differential. There is substantial technical literature in economics that treats the subject of this differential, usually in the form of attempting to explain differing wage levels.[4] Since wages are such a significant portion of income in the United States, that literature is pertinent to our problem and, accordingly, we will attempt to summarize it.

The first source of the North-South differential to be considered is differences in the industrial mix of the two areas. Generally speaking, the South can be characterized as having a heavier preponderance of its labor force working in relatively low wage types of employment.

Consequently, even if southern workers were paid exactly the same wages as northern workers, a gap between the average wage levels in the two regions still would remain. However, this can be adjusted for, and after it is, a residual differential of very substantial proportions persists. Explaining this residual differential is somewhat more difficult. The most sophisticated analysis to date indicates that variations in wage levels between states can be explained by differences in (1) the quantity of physical capital available to each worker, (2) the average level of lifetime educational expenditure per worker (i.e., the quantity of investment in educational human capital), (3) the proportion of non-white employment, (4) the proportion of female employment, and (5) the impact of trade unions on wage levels.[5]

While these variables are all important in explaining interstate variations in wages, they have a differential impact from the standpoint of the North-South disparity. The major point worth noting in this respect is that on a North-South basis there is no significant difference in the availability of physical capital per worker. Thus, this contributes nothing to accounting for the North-South wage differential. The truly significant elements are differences in investment in educational human capital, variations in the level of non-white employment, and the trade union factor.[6] They operate in the following way: The South has less investment in educational human capital, more non-white employment, and less trade unionism. All of these function to produce lower wage levels in the South than in the North.

Two of these factors deserve closer attention. First, the difference in education levels reflects a long standing tendency in the South toward both fewer years of education and lower per pupil expenditures on education. This has been largely a matter of public policy in the southern states, a policy that has apparently reduced wage levels in the area. Second, consistent with our findings in Chapter Six, the high level of non-white (mostly Negro) employment implies a lower average level of endowment with genetic human capital. This has its impact on wages through its effect on average productivity levels (also discussed in Chapter Six). Thus, a significant portion of the North-South wage differential can probably be traced to a factor that may lie outside the area of social control (except through migration of Negroes, which will be discussed later).

The second broad class of regional income differential, urban-rural disparities, has at least two obvious causes, the greater emphasis on relatively low income producing agricultural activity and a smaller average amount of educational human capital in rural areas.[7] Of course, the existence of greater amounts of agricultural activity in rural areas is virtually true by definition. The way in which we determine rural-urban status tends to ensure that agricultural activity will be more dominant in rural areas. Thus, for this to be a meaningful explanation of the urban-rural income differential, we must say something about the reasons for agricultural income being less than non-agricultural.

One of the most persistent phenomena of American economic life has been the lower return to human resources employed in agriculture compared to those used in non-agricultural pursuits. Remarkably, throughout the twentieth century, there has been almost no change in the relative income of agricultural workers in the United States.[8] This has occurred, despite a tremendous movement of human resources out of agriculture into non-agricultural employment. Such stability implies that there is something systematic about the market for human resources in agriculture that leads to the kind of consistent income differential that is observed. Some of the mechanics of that market mechanism will be treated in the next portion of this chapter. Suffice it to say, at this point, that the equilibrium combination of human and non-human resources in this industry implies levels of human resource productivity that are less than those found elsewhere in the economy. Similarly, the lower average level of possession of human capital of the formal education type probably operates to create lower average productivity among the rural population. To these elements will be added a third possible source of urban-rural income differentials, namely, lower levels of genetic human capital in rural areas. However, the specifics of why this may be the case will be postponed until we discuss the impact of migration on income differentials in the next section of this chapter.

Finally, there is the inner city-suburban income gap to explain. Some hint of one of the major sources of intra-metropolitan area income differences has already been provided by the previous remarks about the differing racial mixes of the inner city and the suburbs. The implications of this ought to be obvious by now, namely, a lower average level of genetic human capital in the inner city areas. However, this is not a complete explanation, for it does not account for the income differential between inner city and suburban whites. Such a differential exists, but the straightforward variations in genetic human capital hypothesis is not sufficient here. What is required is a variant of the differential genetic human capital thesis which will be developed shortly. To understand it, we must turn now to a discussion of the relationship between regional income differences and patterns of population migration.

II. THE IMPACT OF MIGRATION ON REGIONAL INCOME DIFFERENCES

American society is characterized by a tremendous amount of movement of individuals between geographic areas. This is not a new phenomenon in the United States. Historically, Americans have been an extremely mobile people, so much so, in fact, that the current volume of movement is probably little different from what it was in

1850.[9] But, what does this have to do with the regional income differences we have been discussing? Simply this: Economic theory suggests that if population and labor force movements between regions are responsive in a positive way to differences in economic advantage, those differentials will tend to be eroded away. This is accomplished by labor resources moving until the ratios of capital to labor are equal in various areas. At this point, wage rates (and income levels) would also be equal.[10]

This is an interesting proposition, but one that would seem to fly in the face of the evidence that has been presented here. For example, a substantial North-South wage differential exists despite the fact that the physical capital/labor ratio in these areas is approximately equal. Further, this happens *despite the fact that there is ample evidence that people are responsive to economic differentials when moving between regions.*[11] How can this be? The explanation lies in the fact that human capital cannot be transported between regions independently of "pure" labor since it is essentially non-transferable between people. This is obviously the case with genetic human capital, but is also true of formal education and/or job training. Once people have received this form of human capital, it is theirs and they cannot transfer the ownership rights to others. Because of this, income equalization between regions through migration of people or physical capital is not likely to occur as long as there are differential regional human capital endowments. The technical aspects of this argument are somewhat involved, but it can be shown unambiguously that this is the case.[12] Consequently, since the South has a lower average level of human capital of both the educational and genetic type (due to its racial mix), there are limits as to how much regional income equalization migration will produce.

So much for the impact of migration on the North-South income differential. Let us turn now to the relationship between migratory flows of people and the urban-rural income disparity. The pattern here has been one of very substantial flows of people from the rural to the urban areas. In particular, the historic flow of people out of agricultural employment has been immense, more than sufficient to adjust to the reduced quantity demanded of agricultural labor that has marked the history of the United States. Yet, the urban-rural income differential persists. Why? As suggested earlier, largely, I suspect, because productivity levels of rural people are consistently less than those of urban residents. The basic reason for this is a selective pattern in migration into and out of rural areas. Roughly, what appears to happen is this: Outmigration from rural to urban areas occurs primarily among the young and especially among the young who possess greater amounts of human capital, both acquired and genetic. This is a rather natural response, for the opportunities to earn the rewards that accrue to the owners of human capital are markedly less in the rural areas. The end result, though, is a progressive deterioration of the human capital component of the rural resource base. The erosion of the level of rural human capital is accelerated by a net immigration of older relatively unsuccessful (in an economic sense) people into agriculture.[13] This merely accentuates the selectivity of the migration process.

The selectivity of migration phenomenon is repeated in the case of the inner city-suburban income differential. Among the typical population of a metropolitan area, the more affluent (and presumably economically "competent") tend to choose to live in the suburbs. Interestingly, there is some evidence to indicate that this occurs independent of race,[14] but due to the inter-racial differences in income levels, the end result is the so-called urban "ghetto," i.e., a much larger proportion of non-whites in the inner city than in the suburbs. This is frequently interpreted as being evidence of "de facto" segregation. However, a substantial amount of the differential racial mixes of the inner city and suburban areas may well reflect the fact that suburban living is essentially an income elastic commodity. To the extent that this is true, the "ghettoization" of metropolitan areas is a function of a selective settlement pattern that groups people according to their income levels.

Since the prime determinant of income levels is the ability to command human resource income and the chief source of differentials in that ability is variations in levels of human capital ownership, the major effect of people being grouped residentially by income levels is typically the concentration of the more economically qualified in the suburbs with the less economically able being relegated to the inner city areas. Thus, suburban residents will tend to have higher average levels of formal education and, on the average, will be better endowed with genetic human capital. In contemporary America, this would occur even in the absence of racial distinctions. However, the racial factor seems to place the problem in an entirely different dimension. It is interesting to speculate whether the term "ghetto" (as currently applied to many inner city areas) would have come into use if it were not for the obvious presence of a disproportionate number of Negroes in these areas. Yet, what we are suggesting here is that the so-called "ghetto" arises largely out of people being residentially grouped according to their ownership of human capital, a process which, according to our previous arguments, operates automatically to ensure a larger proportion of Negroes in the "disadvantaged" areas, i.e., the inner city.

Assuming that the selective migration hypothesis is valid, why has it been essentially a phenomenon of the post-World War II era? The distinction between the suburbs and the inner city is a relatively recent development and requires explanation. Two major factors have contributed to the rapid growth in suburban living in the immediate past. Both have served to relax the constraints that have operated in the past to make the American city a much more compact institution. First, the long term trend toward a shorter work day in the United States culminated in the eight hour work day becoming national policy during the 1930's. The full impact of this was not felt until after World War II when the greater availability of non-work (or "leisure") time made it possible for people to live a substantially greater distance from their work. In effect, the general movement from a longer to a shorter work day creates more leisure time for people and offers them the alternative of using that time for commuting purposes. Apparently, many people have chosen to use their "leisure" time in this fashion, for the practice of commuting substantial distances to work has become commonplace.

Once the trends toward commuting activity became established, a dynamic process was set in motion that has functioned to make it more widespread. First, the increase in the number of commuters created traffic problems for urban officials. In response to this, the high speed expressway and freeway was developed which, in turn, only made it easier for people to commute. Perhaps the prime example of this phenomenon is the Southern California (i.e., Los Angeles) area. Because of the building of the Los Angeles freeway system, the greatest "urban sprawl" in history has been generated. In places, portions of the city of Los Angeles are as much as 25 miles from its center, which means that people living in the same city may reside 50 miles apart. To provide some perspective on the geographic size of Los Angeles, keep in mind that the cities of Baltimore and Washington, D.C., *and all the areas between them* could be placed within the city limits of Los Angeles. Admittedly, Los Angeles is a somewhat special case, but similar growth patterns have been characteristic of most larger American metropolitan areas. In addition, in recent years, another dimension has been included in this dynamic process. Largely because of the migration of the more skilled components of the labor force to the suburbs, industries that use those skills have been relocating in the suburban areas. This simply makes it possible for the suburbs to be extended to even greater distances from the inner city.

The second major contributor to the creation of the inner city-suburban dichotomy has been the sustained period of economic growth that commenced with the onset of World War II. For over 30 years, per capita income levels have been rising consistently which has made it possible for people to afford the costs of living at extended distances from the central city. Typically, the cost of the suburban housing package exceeds that of the inner city. Add to this commuting costs and the like and it is easy to see why, on the average, residing in the suburbs is more costly than average inner city living.[15] Given the relative expensiveness of suburban living vis-a-vis the inner city, the rapid growth in income levels in recent years has simply served to accelerate the movement to the suburbs or, as it is sometimes called, the "flight from the cities."[16]

III. URBAN AND RURAL "GHETTOES"

Let us put our discussion of geographic variations in income and poverty differentials into some type of broad perspective. The primary effect of the type of migration and settlement patterns that we have observed has been the creation of clearly definable geographic groupings of individuals according to their economic status. This is particularly so in the case of the urban-rural and suburban-inner city living patterns. What has happened over the course of the past quarter century is the virtual elimination of residential areas that are a microcosm of American society. In their place has been substituted extremely homogeneous groupings of people. This has had some interesting side effects. The most important among them are (1) a loss of perspective with respect to the nature of American society and (2) a concentration of the problems of income maintenance for the poor in particular geographic locations.

The loss of perspective arises out of people not having readily available in their everyday surroundings a basis of comparison of economic status among the population. Thus, those who are reared in relatively affluent and homogeneous residential areas have little insight into the range of differences among people and, ultimately, the sources of poverty. Similarly, those living in the equally homogeneous, but non-affluent, areas lack an understanding of the ultimate sources of higher income levels. At a time when residential communities were more representative of the variety of human talents, people had a better appreciation of the sources of economic differentials. At present, though, that appreciation has been significantly altered by the homogeneity of their residential surroundings. In the place of an understanding of the reasons for income differentials come cliches such as the concept of the "ghetto" which suggest that differentials in economic status are institutionally imposed on selected groups of people in American society. Not surprisingly, such feelings appear to be strongest among those whose exposure to the range of economic experience is the least, namely, the relatively young reared in families whose income places them either in the upper or lower tail of the income distribution.

The economic stratification of the population also produces a restructuring of the burden of public expenditures for income maintenance for the poor (i.e., public welfare costs). What now exist are governmental units that contain a disproportionately large number of the poor in our society. This produces substantial financial problems for these governmental units. For example, the phenomenon of the metropolitan government facing a financial crisis due to welfare and education costs is commonplace. Were it not for state governments providing assistance to these communities in order to equalize the burden of welfare, many metropolitan governmental units simply could not survive financially. Even so, the problem of these agencies of government is complicated by the fact that very recent evidence indicates that people in general, and especially Negroes, are more prone to migrate to areas that have relatively high levels of welfare payments.[17] Thus, one of the effects of states and municipalities being more munificent in the provision of welfare benefits is an increase in their case load through migration.

While on the subject of responsiveness of people to the availability of welfare payment type income, it is worth noting that there is ample evidence that providing people with welfare payment income tends to increase welfare case loads.[18] This is the familiar question of whether there are negative work incentive effects associated with the provision of transfer payment income. The discussion of Chapters Seven and Eight is largely predicated on the existence of such effects and the available evidence is consistent with them. Beyond this, though, other data indicate that such effects are present. For example, one study finds that the elasticity of the welfare case load with respect to the level of welfare benefits is about one-half, i.e., a one percent increase in welfare benefits will produce a one-half of one percent increase in the number of people on welfare.[19]

Till recently, the evidence supporting the existence of negative work incentive effects was of the indirect type. To remedy that, the Federal Government commissioned a massive "negative income tax experiment" in the New York-New Jersey area intended to determine the effects on work activity of providing people with transfer payment income. The design of the experiment is straightforward: A number of relatively poor people have been enrolled in a program that provides them with varying amounts of transfer payment income that has no work restrictions attached to it. The income is guaranteed for a three year period. At the same time, a matched "control" group has been selected which does not receive transfer income. By comparing the behavior of the two groups, it should be possible to infer something about the impact of transfer payment income on work activity among the poor.

There are faults in the design of the experiment with the major one being the limited time period (three years) for which the transfer income is provided. Because of this limit, people may tend to regard the income as being transitory in nature and not fully adjust their consumption patterns to its presence. Keep in mind that substituting leisure for income because of the availability of transfer income essentially represents a change in consumption patterns. More leisure is bought in the place of other goods. Despite this shortcoming, though, the first results of the experiment are quite enlightening.[20] They have been widely ballyhooed by the agency bureaucrats as indicating no negative impact on work activity as the result of making transfer income available to people. Unfortunately, this is one of the grossest misinterpretations of data that I have encountered. It is based on no apparent change in the amount of work related income received by the experimental group compared to the control group. This is true, *but* it occurs because of an inexplicably large increase in hourly wage rates among those enrolled in the experimental group.[21] The actual *physical* amount of work activity forthcoming from members of the experimental group falls significantly relative to the control group. And, of course, this is what negative work incentive effects are all about, the impact on the physical volume of work effort forthcoming. Lest there be concern that the relative increase in the money wage rates of the experimental group introduces a bias in this direction, rest assured. Any interpretation of the data that argues that higher money wage rates will reduce work activity must admit that negative work incentive effects will follow from giving people unrestricted transfer payment income.[22]

At this point, we can begin to grasp more fully the dynamics of so-called "ghettoes" in our society. A number of factors explain their existence, but a major one is the pattern of migration of the American population. In general, people migrate toward what they perceive to be economic opportunity and this takes them out of the rural and in to the urban areas. Further, the migration is probably selective in the sense that those with the greatest amounts of genetic and acquired human capital are best able to avail themselves of the economic opportunity offered by the urban areas. Once in the urban areas, this pattern is repeated, only on a smaller scale. The more affluent (i.e., those with a greater capacity to command economic rewards) choose to live in the suburbs while those who are less economically able are left in the inner city. The result is a relative lack of both genetic and acquired human capital among inner city residents and a heavy concentration of Negroes in these areas. Since the inner city population is low income almost by definition, the incidence of welfare payments is much greater and the financial burden on the metropolitan governments becomes almost unbearable. As relief comes from external sources (federal and state), there is a tendency for individual welfare payments to rise and this induces a further increase in the welfare case load, either through people with marginally low levels of work income shifting out of the labor force (particularly women with dependent children) or because of inmigration attracted by the higher welfare benefits.[23]

The net result of this entire process is awesome to behold. On the one hand, there are the rural areas which have lost probably the most economically capable element of their population. In effect, in many cases, the process creates the rural equivalent of the "ghetto," i.e., a concentrated group of the relatively poor. These rural "ghettoes" are frequently overlooked, but they are an integral part of the process by which economic stratification of residential areas occurs in contemporary America. Counterposed to the rural "ghettoes" are the urban "ghettoes," largely non-white, largely lacking in human capital, and largely dependent on the welfare mechanism for income maintenance. It is from this set of circumstances that the notion of an "urban crisis" arises.

One clarifying point should be made. The pattern of responses to economic stimuli that have been described in this chapter will cause some to be critical of the poor on the grounds that they are "lazy," "shiftless," or "to blame for their own circumstances." This is not appropriate. The behavioral patterns we have described are quite consistent with the economist's concept of maximizing behavior by individuals in the labor market. There is more than casual evidence to indicate that people in general respond to economic incentives in the fashion suggested by economic theory.[24] Why, then, should it be reprehensible on the part of the poor to react in the same manner? Being poor neither makes one any more or less "moral" and "responsible" in their behavior. The fact that the poor act in a fashion that seems to generate severe problems for the society says more about the type of income maintenance systems we have developed than it does about the "morality" of the poor.

IV. CONCLUSIONS

What have we really said in this chapter? Primarily, it has been argued that the problems associated with regional variations in levels of income and poverty have their roots in the dynamics of population movement in the United States. In a systematic fashion, people are sorted and categorized and the end result is the economic stratification of residential areas that gives rise to the institution of the "ghetto," both urban and rural. Within these areas, the population generally is not only low income, but relatively poorly qualified (in a human capital sense) to make any appreciable progress towards remedying their situation. And, those who do usually leave the area which further denudes it of the human capital component of its resource base. The end product is a society of the disadvantaged, a society that is heavily reliant on income maintenance programs, which is simply a fancy phrase to describe the "welfare system." Of course, complicating the problem is the racial mix of the urban ghettoes (which has already been explained). This adds a social and political dimension to the problem of great complexity.

But, what can we do in a policy sense to deal with this problem? Very little, if our analysis is correct. Short of regulating and controlling the mobility patterns of the American people, there is not much that can be done to prevent the type of residential economic stratification that gives rise to the ghetto. Certainly, so-called "open-housing" will help, but I really suspect that housing discrimination is only a minor part of the dynamic that gives rise to the ghetto. What is really critical are the patterns of population movements and these have shown no tendency

toward marked change in recent years. This is one of the most intriguing aspects of the so-called "urban problem." Despite all the
reports of how desparately bad living conditions are in our large
metropolitan areas, the migration to them continues. Just think what
the migration would be if we heeded the pleas of the nation's mayors
and spent billions upon billions of dollars refurbishing our cities. The
fascinating question, though, is why this continued migration, given
the crime, pollution, congestion, etc., that are associated with urban
living. The answer is simple: The lure of economic opportunity is
overwhelmingly strong. People, in general, are only weakly responsive
to these other factors, their protestations to the contrary not
withstanding.[25] Certainly, they would prefer a pleasant place to live,
but not if it means much of a decrease in their level of income. Consequently, at least for the present, the phenomenon of residential
economic stratification of our population, and all the problems that go
with it, appears to be a fairly permanent fixture of the American social
landscape.

FOOTNOTES

[1]Of all Negro families living in metropolitan areas, 78 percent live in the
central city. Among whites, this percentage is 39. As a result, 20
percent of central city families and only three percent of non-central
city families are Negro. Source: *Current Population Reports, P-60
Series.*

[2]Note from footnote 1 that four-fifths of central city families are white.
The suburbs may be predominantly white, but so is the central city.

[3]*Equality of Educational Opportunity, op. cit.*

[4]See, in particular, Scully, Gerald W., "Interstate Wage Differentials: A
Cross-Section Analysis," *American Economic Review*, December 1969,
pp. 757-773.

[5]For details, see Scully, "Interstate Wage Differentials," *op. cit.*

[6]It has been pointed out to me that there may be something of a contradiction between our recognizing that differences in the average
quantity of acquired human capital of the educational form are an
important source of regional wage differentials and the arguments of
Chapter Six, which emphasized the importance of differential endowments of genetic human capital as a source of income differentials.
To clarify this point, I note first that in Chapter Six, our concern was
focused on explaining an income differential that apparently could not
be accounted for by differences in educational levels (particularly
quantitative differences). It is at this point that the concept of differential endowment with genetic human capital enters the picture. In
no way do we argue that if there exist two groups with the same
average level of genetic human capital, differential possession of

acquired human capital will not affect their income. On the other hand, we strongly suggest that if two groups have similar levels of ownership of acquired human capital, differential endowment with genetic human capital will produce income differences. The latter is roughly the case of Chapter Six, although it can be maintained that an educational gap between blacks and whites still remains. However, in this chapter, we are discussing a situation where we have controlled for the major source of differences in the average quantity of genetic human capital (the racial mix of the population). Therefore, essentially we are comparing two groups that may be assumed to have roughly equal levels of endowment with genetic human capital. In such a case, there is nothing contradictory about observing that ownership of acquired human capital has a significant impact on wage differentials. One further point: In the basic study of regional wage differentials that has been cited, almost two-thirds of the observed North-South wage differential can be explained on the basis of the differential racial composition of the population. Thus, compared to the racial factor, variations in acquired human capital are of smaller importance as an explanation of the North-South wage differential.

[7] Median school years completed among the population aged 25 years and over are 10.7 for the rural farm population, 11.2 for the rural non-farm population, and 12.2 for the urban population. Source: United States Census, *General Social and Economic Characteristics, op. cit.*, Table 75.

[8] For evidence of this phenomenon, see Bachmura, F.T., "Migration and Factor Adjustment in Lower Mississippi Valley Agriculture: 1940-1950," *Journal of Farm Economics*, November 1956, pp. 1024-1042; Bishop, C.E., "Economic Development and Adjustments in Southeastern Low Income Agriculture," *Journal of Farm Economics*, December 1954, pp. 1146-1158; and Hathaway, D.E., "Migration from Agriculture: The Historical Experience and Its Meaning," *American Economic Review*, May 1960, pp. 403-412.

[9] Data presented in Gallaway, Lowell E., and Vedder, Richard K., "Mobility of Native Americans," *Journal of Economic History*, September 1971, pp. 613-649 show that in 1850, 24.2 percent of all native born Americans lived in a state other than their state of birth, while as of the 1970 Census, the percentage was 27.9. Source: United States Census, *General Social and Economic Characteristics, op. cit.*, Table 69. This would not seem to square with some of the recent commentaries suggesting that there has been a tremendous increase in the amount of mobility in the United States. For example, see Toffler, Alvin, *Future Shock*, New York: Random House, 1970.

[10] This assumes that regional production functions are similar.

[11] For example, see Gallaway and Vedder, "Mobility of Native Americans," *op. cit.*, and Gallaway, *Manpower Economics, op. cit.*, Chapter 4.

[12] This is shown in Gallaway, Lowell E., and Cebula, Richard J., "The Impact of Property Rights in Human Capital on Regional Factor Proportions," *Zeitschrift fur Nationalokonomie*, No. 4, 1972.

[13] For details, see my "Mobility of Hired Agricultural Labor," *Journal of Farm Economics*, February 1967, pp. 32-52.

[14] See my "Urban Decay and the Labor Market," *Quarterly Review of Economics and Business*, Winter 1967, pp. 7-16.

[15] By "expensive," we mean the cost of the total package of suburban living. Per unit of living space of a given quality, suburban living is cheaper than that in the inner city. However, the typical "package" of suburban living involves more living space and higher quality accommodations. Thus, the higher cost.

[16] Differentials in the general quality of life in the suburbs may also contribute to the outmovement of people. For example, differences in pollution levels, crime rates, etc., tend to make suburban living more attractive. Of course, this was substantially the case *before* the tremendous outmovement of recent years. This suggests that perhaps the critical element in producing the "flight from the cities" is the relaxation of the constraints that traditionally have held people in the cities.

[17] This evidence is presented in Kohn, Robert; Vedder, Richard K.; and Cebula, Richard J., "The Determinants of Interstate Migration by Race, 1965-1970," Research Paper No. 161, Ohio University Department of Economics, 1973.

[18] See, e.g., Brehm, C.T., and Saving, T.R., "The Demand for General Assistance Payments," *American Economic Review*, December 1964, pp. 1002-1018.

[19] Kasper, Hirschel, "Welfare Payments and Work Incentive: Some Determinants of the Rates of General Assistance Payments," *Journal of Human Resources*, Winter 1968, pp. 86-110.

[20] These are reported in *Preliminary Results of the New Jersey Graduated Work Incentive Experiment*, Office of Economic Opportunity, February 18, 1970. A much more judicious appraisal of the results is contained in Watts, Harold, "Mid Experiment Report on Basic Labor Supply Response," Institute for Research on Poverty, University of Wisconsin, Madison, Wisconsin.

[21] It is possible that this extra large increase is the result of people systematically under reporting wage levels at the time of enrollment in the program. Once they discover that there really are not penalties

associated with receiving work income, the experimental group may then report more accurately, while the control group continues to under report.

22 For higher money wage rates to reduce work activity, the income effect associated with them must dominate the substitution effect. If this is the case, the impact of transfer payment income must be to reduce work activity.

23 We would expect the shifting out of the labor force to be more prevalent among women due to greater attempts to enforce work requirements against men.

24 Again, see *Manpower Economics, op cit.*, Chapter 4.

25 One recent study indicates that migration flows between metropolitan areas are relatively insensitive to such things as air pollution and the like. See Cebula, Richard J., and Vedder, Richard K., "A Note on Migration, Economic Opportunity, and the Quality of Life," *Journal of Regional Science*, forthcoming.

A PUBLIC POLICY TOWARDS POVERTY

CHAPTER 10

Thomas Carlyle once described "classical" economics as "the dismal science."[1] In large part, his characterization was motivated by (1) the apparent inability of economics to prescribe clear paths towards improving the human condition and (2) its tendency to suggest that there is something natural and unavoidable about misery.[2] At times, I must confess, some of the conclusions reached in this volume have caused me to ponder Carlyle's description of economics. Clearly, there runs through much of what we have said the impression that differentials in income levels are the "natural" state of affairs, arising primarily out of differential ownership of human capital, both of the acquired and genetic type. In particular, the heavy emphasis on the importance of differentials in endowment with genetic human capital tends to support the notion of a "natural" tendency towards inequality in a society's income distribution. Since this has extremely significant public policy implications, let us summarize the evidence on this count.

I. THE NATURALNESS OF INCOME INEQUALITY

Two major factors contribute to the "natural" character of income differentials in the United States. First, there is the already noted impact of differences in the levels of genetic human capital possessed by individuals in our society. It is our contention (especially in Chapter Five) that the importance of this source of variation in the level of economic rewards received by people has been consistently underestimated.[3] In fact, it may well be that the primary producer of differences in levels of human resource earnings is variations in genetic human capital endowment rather than differential levels of ownership of acquired human capital. All that much investment in acquired human capital does is determine the particular occupation in which someone will collect economic rent on his genetic human capital. Certainly, in the case of some occupational callings, the minimal requirement is not a particular amount of acquired human capital, but a certain level of genetic human capital. Without the latter, the acquired human capital would be virtually worthless to the society and would be rewarded accordingly. In fact, in certain extreme cases, lack of the necessary genetic human capital simply would preclude acquisition of the acquired human capital that is associated with an occupation.

If genetic human capital is as important in determining differences in human resource income as we have argued, the fact that income derived from the sale of human resources is such a dominant portion of overall income and contributes so substantially to the inequality of income distribution emphasizes the significance of genetic human capital as a source of "naturalness" of income differentials. The relative importance of human resource income is the second major factor that contributes to the "natural" character of the overall income distribution. Remember, almost six-sevenths of personal income is of the human resource type. Consequently, anything that contributes to inequality in the distribution of that income is critically important in explaining inequality in the distribution of all income.

Thus far, we have been using the term "natural" without specifying exactly what we mean by it. From the context in which the expression has been employed, its approximate meaning is reasonably clear. "Natural" sources of income differentials are those that are non-environmentally determined and, therefore, are not susceptible to control through altering the social and economic institutions of the nation. This is precisely what is implied by the concept of genetic human capital, endowments of which cannot be controlled short of widespread genetic engineering. In a free society, that does not seem to be a viable policy alternative and, consequently, will be disregarded.

The apparently "natural" character of income differentials in the United States may seem to suggest the kind of inevitability in economic affairs that prompted Carlyle's dismay. However, there is a fundamental difference here. Carlyle's concern was directed at an economics that not only exuded inevitability, but implied that the best that the masses of the population could expect was existence at the level of minimum physical subsistence. By contrast, the "naturalness" that we have been discussing refers to relative inequality of economic status. There is nothing to suggest that people will be driven naturally to the very margin of physical existence. Rather, all may be well above the level of physical subsistence, but some will be much more advantageously placed than others for reasons that are "natural" in character. Thus, the conclusions we have reached in this volume are not nearly as "dismal" as they might seem at first glance.

While the picture we have sketched does not contain the grinding inevitability of misery that marked classical economics, it does indicate that there are distinct limits to what can be done in the realm of public policy. Specifically, if income differentials are largely the result of market valuations of genetic, i.e., "natural" differences between people, there is little that can be done from the standpoint of public policy to equalize income distribution through approaches intended to augment the human capital of low income individuals. Thus, emphasis on increasing formal education, job retraining, and the like, are not apt to produce substantial improvements in the relative economic status of low income people. And, therein lies a fundamental dilemma. Basically, the United States is a society that embraces and accepts the "work ethic." That ethic emphasizes the desirability of obtaining income through the medium of work activity, i.e., by selling one's human resources in the labor market. Therefore, the conclusion that public policy approaches that attempt to augment the quantity and quality of the human resources that people have available for income earning purposes are likely to be relatively ineffective, implies that greater income equality can be obtained only by resorting to policies that run counter to a widely held precept of the society. For example, simply note the increasing concern being expressed in our political life about the magnitude of the "welfare problem." This merely reflects a certain unwillingness among the general population to supply people with transfer payment (non-work) income on a large scale basis.

The dilemma we have outlined is a critical one in several respects. While the validity of the "work ethic" has come under attack in recent years by elements of the so-called "counter-culture," it is still a dominant force in American life. Consequently, the only policy alternative, with respect to income distribution in the United States, that appears to be reasonably consistent with the social values of the society seems to be one of accepting the existing degree of inequality as being workable. Translated into a public policy with respect to poverty, this means that if poverty is defined in a relative sense, a la Fuchs, the existing level of poverty is acceptable. The alternative would seem to be to define poverty in absolute terms and then rely on economic growth to reduce the observed level of poverty. Now, if this begins to sound again like Carlyle's "dismal science," I must agree, with one significant reservation. Whereas the classical economics implied the inevitability of absolute poverty, what we have argued suggests the inevitability of relative poverty, unless the society is willing to engage in large scale programs (involving substantial pure transfers of income) that run contrary to its broad value structure.[4]

II. RACIAL ASPECTS OF INCOME INEQUALITY

The basic dilemma confronting public policy makers in the poverty area is nowhere more acute than when dealing with the question of racial differences in the incidence of poverty. This is the area where our analysis probably produces its most controversial results. The major thrust of our argument is that the differential incidence of poverty among the dominant group of non-whites, i.e., Negroes, may well be lower levels of productivity that are the result of racial differences in endowment with genetic human capital. This is a devastating finding, particularly with respect to those public policy approaches that are based philosophically on environmental explanations (mostly "discrimination") for racial income differentials. These tend to emphasize either augmenting the acquired human capital of Negroes vis-a-vis whites or "rooting out" every vestige of "discrimination" in the society. If one accepts the arguments presented in Chapters Five and Six, it is clear that attacking the problem of racial income and poverty differentials through these methods is not likely to produce any substantial improvements in the relative economic position of Negroes in the United States in the future.

This leaves either the device of transfer payments to Negroes or enforced "reverse discrimination" against whites sufficient to overcome the natural disadvantages Negroes bring to the labor market. Both of these are inconsistent with certain rather widely held positions, *viz.*, the aforementioned "work ethic" and the notion that economic rewards should reflect "merit." Consequently, the fundamental dilemma of a lack of consistency between public policy and social values is again present. Further complicating matters is the fact that one of the policy approaches, transfer payment income to low income individuals, may have the negative effect of separating Negroes even further from the mainstream of American economic and social life. Having a significantly larger proportion of Negroes than whites receiving transfer payment income may contribute markedly to the impression that Negroes and whites exist in markedly different worlds. In short, it can do much to create and perpetuate an image of a polarized two-class society.

One other aspect of the transfer payment approach also needs to be noted. Basically, one can conceive of a broad program of providing the relatively poor with transfer payment income. This would automatically redound to the favor of Negroes, due to their disproportionate representation in the ranks of the low income population. However, it would only be of assistance to Negroes who qualified as being poor according to some population wide definition. It would do nothing for Negroes who have incomes above the level necessary in order to be eligible for the transfer income. For example, if transfer income were provided to pull all families up to the present "poverty line," the median income of Negro families would not be affected. Thus, the basic problem of Negro-white income differentials would remain.[5]

What about the possibility of "reverse discrimination" against whites and in favor of Negroes? An interesting possibility; one that, in fact, we have been pursuing to a certain extent in recent years. Certainly, if our analysis of the sources of the Negro-white income differential is valid, the tremendous pressure for "equal employment opportunity," which usually translates into racial employment quotas, represents "reverse discrimination." However, as presently constituted, insistence on equal employment opportunity does not *consciously* represent a policy of "reverse discrimination," for it is motivated by the belief that discrimination against Negroes is widespread. In only one respect is there currently conscious "reverse discrimination" against whites. This comes in that nebulous area of "affirmative action" programs. As administered by government agencies (particularly at the Federal level), "affirmative action" means consciously seeking Negro employees in preference to whites. This smacks of deliberate "reverse discrimination," although it has frequently been defended on the grounds that Negroes have less access to labor market information than whites.[6]

Whether "reverse discrimination" actually exists in our society is not the critical issue. What is important, though, is whether such discrimination would be viable as a long term instrument of public policy. In one sense I suspect it is. Realistically, what I have argued in this book represents a distinct minority view within the world of scholarship and political opinion. When one finds himself in that position, he does not expect to transform the world overnight. That is an illusion that only extreme youth can sustain. Consequently, I fully expect the conventional wisdom to continue to dominate public policy and this is sufficient in itself to make "reverse discrimination" viable for a substantial period, since that wisdom provides a philosophical basis for such discrimination. However, if my analysis is correct, I would also anticipate that implementing the present equal employment opportunity policies will create such stresses and strains within the social fabric that eventually it will prove to be totally unworkable as an instrument of social policy.

One remaining facet of public policy with respect to the Negro-white income and poverty differentials must be discussed in order to complete our coverage of the subject. Assuming the worst, which is that I am correct, there still remains a long term solution to the dilemma of how to eliminate racial economic differentials. It involves creating a world in which "color" truly does not matter, by eliminating "color" from the society. This can be done through the device of racial intermarriage, which would progressively destroy racial distinctions while also removing the differences in genetic endowments that we have argued are the primary source of the Negro-white income differential. While this may be the ultimate solution to the problem of racial economic differentials, it is not clear that it is an easily acceptable one for either race. On the one hand, there are whites who would find widespread racial intermarriage objectionable. We are assuming, of course, that such marriages would be entered into voluntarily. Even so, the displeasure of a portion of the white community will operate to impose social costs on such couples and substantially reduce the likelihood of such marriages.

Similarly, given the recent tendency among militant Negroes to emphasize black awareness and black traditions, a substantial number of Negroes would also object to "mixed" marriages. Not all Negroes would wish to see racial distinctions blurred and eventually destroyed. Perhaps the best testimonial to that attitude is the widely trumpeted slogan "black is beautiful." This is an attempt to emphasize racial differences, not mute them. Such opposition to racial intermarriage from members of the Negro community would also impose costs on those couples who entered into such unions. Again, this would reduce the probability of intermarriage. Thus, it well could be that this ultimate solution to the problem of racial economic differentials will be a "long time coming."

III. EQUAL OPPORTUNITY FOR WOMEN

We turn now to the question of public policy in the area of providing equal economic opportunity for women. Here, we find a somewhat different situation than that encountered in the case of racial economic differentials. Again, there is evidence that at least a portion of the difference between the economic rewards available to men and women is the result of productivity differentials between men and women. However, there is also evidence of the existence of pure discrimination against women. This combination of factors places women at a distinct economic disadvantage relative to men and creates an issue to be considered by the makers of public policy. To put the problem of the relative economic status of women in perspective, however, it should be realized that, in part, the differential between income levels of families headed by a man and families headed by a woman reflects the tendency of female heads of families to voluntarily substitute a combination of leisure and transfer payment income for work related income. Thus, at least a portion of their relatively adverse money income position represents a preference for non-work activity and is arrived at freely. Nevertheless, substantial problems of income maintenance and poverty elimination remain for these families.

From the public policy standpoint, the alternatives seem to be several: (1) pressure to provide equal employment opportunity for women in an effort to eliminate the discrimination portion of the income differential they face, (2) insuring that investment in the acquired form of human capital is similar for both men and women, and (3) providing transfer payment income to women who are heads of families in order to insure their economic well-being. Our present policy approach is a mixture of these and has yielded what many people would regard as less than satisfactory results.

First, let us look at the efforts to achieve equal employment opportunity for women. Our analysis suggests some need for efforts of this type. However, on the basis of the activities of those who administer these policies, one suspects that they will not be content with anything short of evidence that all male-female economic differentials have been eliminated. As we have seen, achievement of that goal would

require our ignoring certain economic realities that appear to give rise
to legitimate (i.e., productivity produced) differences between men and
women as inputs into the productive processes of the society. Admittedly, it is difficult for those administering equal employment
opportunity programs to operate with the degree of control that our
results suggest would be necessary, particularly since the relative
quantitative magnitudes of the discriminatory and non-discriminatory
portions of male-female economic differentials are not precisely known
for a wide variety of employments. A difficult task is involved here,
but, even so, excessive zeal on the part of program administrators could
have the effect of producing what amounts to "reverse discrimination"
in favor of women.[7] And, one must admit that excessive zeal is a rather
common trait among those who administer government programs that
involve an element of social reform in their mission.

The second broad policy approach to male-female economic differentials, equalization of investment in human capital, is most emphasized by groups that are concerned about equal access for women to
the types of training that are necessary for entry into specific occupations. There can really be no serious question raised (except by the
more paranoiac of the Women's Liberation types) about the availability
to women of the general forms of educational human capital that are
produced in this society. As to specific types of training, though, it is
much more difficult to say. Since advanced training in the occupations
in question is largely in the hands of men, I suspect there is some
tendency for those supervising such training to regard women with a
somewhat jaundiced eye. Part of this skeptical attitude towards women
is undoubtedly a matter of prejudice, but a part may also be the
product of factors similar to those discussed earlier (in Chapter Seven),
when we treated the problem an employer faces when deciding whether
to provide on-the-job-training for women. The basic problem is the
expected return from investing time and effort in the training of
women. This has nothing at all to do with the capacity of women to
absorb such training. That is not an issue. However, there is the matter
of the probability that a woman will actively pursue a profession once
she receives the necessary training. Women have an option that is not
as available to men, namely, the role of the housewife. The possibility of
their exercising that option on a full time basis reduces the probability
of their engaging in an occupation as actively as a man. Due to this,
those who supervise advanced training may be less likely to take
women seriously since they would prefer to concentrate on those more
apt to engage actively in the type of activity for which they are being
trained.

A word of clarification: Nothing that we have said is intended to
suggest that women should not engage in the full variety of occupational callings that exist in the society. However, it is designed to
suggest that, on the average, women may be less interested in these

activities than men. Whether advocates of "equality for women" like it or not, many women do not wish to be "liberated." I would not presume to criticize these women for holding these attitudes, just as I would not presume to find fault with the "liberated woman's" occupational preference function. I do think, though, that it is somewhat presumptuous for the liberated woman to argue for public policies that are based on an assumption that all women have the same occupational preferences as their liberated sisters. This is exactly what they frequently do when they calculate percentages of women employed in various occupations without considering the differential supply of women interested in those occupations. Their basic premise is that the smaller supply of women for some of the more prestigious occupations is indicative of male chauvinist exclusion. However, an alternative explanation is that many women voluntarily restrict their supply of labor to certain occupations due to the demands those callings make on the individuals engaging in them. Again, though, the argument is made that this is only because the dominant male world "conditions" them so that they do not "know any better." As noted earlier, there is simply no logical way to deal with that mode of tautological discourse. What it presumes is an "elitist" female establishment that is entitled by virtue of its great perceptiveness to speak for all women.

What this all means is that the evidence that a smaller percentage of women than men receive specialized training for specific occupations (particularly the more prestigious professional type activities) is not a conclusive indication that women are "discriminated" against unfairly from the standpoint of having access to certain significant forms of acquired human capital. That kind of evidence is interesting, but does not necessarily imply what the advocates of equal opportunity for women argue it does. Again, what this suggests is that formulating public policy on the basis of some of the more common "women's rights" arguments may well result in "reverse discrimination" in favor of women.

The last phase of public policy designed to deal with the problem of the economic status of women is the provision of direct transfer payment income, particularly to women who are heads of families. This has some intriguing implications. First, as we have already pointed out, the availability of such income has had a tendency to reduce the amount of work activity among women. This once more raises the question of a possible conflict between a set of social values that emphasizes the virtues of work activity and the desire to provide at least a minimum level of income for the families involved. However, in this case, the dilemma is not nearly as acute as that encountered when dealing with racial economic differences. There are probably at least two reasons for this. First, the awareness of the magnitude of the problem of the economic status of this group is substantially less than in the case of non-whites.[8] Second, there is probably a tendency for the society as a whole to look with more favor on female heads of household remaining at home to supervise the rearing of their children. Consequently, the negative connotations associated with providing female heads of household with transfer payment income are substantially softened.

Collectively, the public policy alternatives available to deal with the problem of male-female income and poverty differentials seem to offer more palatable possibilities than those encountered in the instance of racial economic differences. Perhaps the more strongly positive aspect of the contemporary scene in this respect is the apparent ability of present income maintenance schemes to induce female heads of household to voluntarily reduce their work activity. At the least, this suggests that the welfare of these women has been improved over what it would have been if they had continued to rely on work related income to sustain themselves. Also on the positive side is the fact that since there is evidence of discrimination against women, policies such as promoting equal employment opportunity for women do have some chance of improving their economic status. However, there is a negative aspect to things, namely, the likelihood that overzealous implementing of equal rights for women type policies is likely to produce some "reverse discrimination" in favor of women. All in all, though, it seems possible to live reasonably satisfactorily with the set of policy alternatives available in this area.

IV. ECONOMIC POLICY TOWARDS THE AGED

If there is one single portion of public policy toward poverty and income maintenance that can be considered to be eminently successful, it is probably the manner in which we have chosen to deal with the problem of income maintenance for the aged. This may seem to be a strange statement, considering the frequency of allegations to the effect that there is a "crisis" situation where income maintenance for the aged is concerned. However, for the reasons that are set forth in detail in Chapter Eight, we do not accept the rationale that is set forth to support the "crisis" philosophy. In fact, we would argue exactly the opposite, i.e., that the relative economic status of the aged has actually been improving in recent years. To recapitulate, it appears that (1) the primary effect of systematically providing the aged with transfer payment income through the Social Security system has been to enable them voluntarily to substitute leisure for work and (2) judging by the behavior of old age benefits under Social Security relative to the Bureau of Labor Statistics Moderate Living Standard budget for retired couples and relative to the level of wages in the economy as a whole, real living standards among the aged have been rising more rapidly than those for the entire country. Both of these phenomena lead to a relative improvement in the broad social welfare position of the aged.

This is not to say that all is perfect with respect to public policy concerning income maintenance for the aged. If our Social Security system is viewed as an "insurance" approach to providing income to the elderly, one can seriously question the wisdom in a free society of mandatory participation in the system. Why not let people choose for themselves whether they wish to contribute to the Social Security system or employ those funds elsewhere (either for consumption or investment purposes). However, this criticism is probably not appropriate since, as the Social Security system has developed, it is clearly not an "insurance" type system. The "insurance" aspect of Social Security is a polite myth that is perpetuated to placate legislators and others who would be apoplectic if they realized what our present Social Security system really is, namely, a reasonably orderly way of transferring income from the non-aged to the aged through the device of a wage tax.[9] Essentially, the various benefits generated by the Social Security system belong in the same class as any other public transfer payment of the general welfare type, except that (1) they are not financed out of the general receipts of the Federal Treasury and (2) they are available as a matter of right and, within broad limits, a "need" for the payments does not have to be demonstrated.[10] Once this is recognized, it becomes clear that Social Security benefits should be treated as a commodity that is provided collectively, rather than as a privately purchased good, because, as a society, we feel they are desirable. In short, there are "public good" dimensions to the Social Security system.

There is one other aspect of the current approach to economic problems among the aged that is somewhat disturbing. This is the tendency for some of the strongest supporters of the present system to depict it as a failure in order to strengthen the argument for a further extension of it. We discussed this in Chapter Eight, but it deserves re-emphasis. In its extreme form, the argument goes that despite the great increase in the availability of transfer payment income to the aged, their economic status has been deteriorating rapidly and, consequently, it is necessary to increase the level of transfer payments even further. Of course, this ignores the fact that there is a consistent negative relationship between receipt of transfer payment income and the amount of work related income received by the aged. If the combined effect of these is really to worsen the economic position of the aged, then it would seem unwise to increase Social Security benefits further. If past experience is an appropriate guide, this would simply worsen things for the aged. However, this is nonsense. Making Social Security benefits available to the aged has not worsened their economic position and those who imply that it has are distorting the actual state of affairs. In the process, they may well hamper rather than assist efforts to formulate public policy towards economic problems of the elderly.

V. TOWARDS A COHERENT PUBLIC POLICY

A volume such as this should end on some sort of positive note and we will do our best in this respect. The primary problem we face in the area of public policy towards poverty is the resolution of the basic conflict between the "work ethic" in American Society and provision of minimal income levels. Dealing with this dilemma has been the major objective of most anti-poverty programs over the past decade. Such approaches as job retraining, improved educational opportunity for the poor, and equal employment opportunity legislation have all been aimed at reducing the incidence of poverty by either eliminating barriers to job opportunity or by augmenting the quantities of acquired human capital possessed by the poor. Attacking the poverty problem in this fashion implies a committment to reducing income differentials and eliminating poverty by methods designed to draw people into the mainstream of American economic life. More recently, though, there seems to be a greater emphasis in public debate on pure transfer payment approaches to providing general minimum income maintenance. This is perhaps best illustrated by the extent to which this issue arose during the 1972 presidential campaign.

The greater recent emphasis on pure transfer payment programs probably reflects the somewhat spotty performance of the alternative policies in reducing poverty. As our analysis has suggested, during the decade of the 1960's, the major contributor to reducing the poverty rate was sustained economic growth. Further, other portions of this volume provide a basis for expecting relatively little from approaches that emphasize eliminating discrimination and augmenting the acquired human capital of the poor. Neither of these can do anything to eliminate the income differentials dictated by inequality in the distribution of genetic human capital. Therefore, it is not surprising that the performance of specific poverty programs during the 1960's was not spectacular.

At this point, our basic problem may seem to be insoluble. If little can be accomplished by anti-discrimination and human capital augmenting approaches, what is left other than pure income supplementation through transfer payments, with all that implies for violation of the "work ethic?" Elsewhere, I am on record as advocating a policy approach designed to provide both income supplementation and involvement in the mainstream of American economic activity.[11] This plan calls for providing employers with a subsidy in return for their employing low productivity workers. It is possible to design a scheme that will determine whether an individual is low productivity on the basis of his past earnings levels (which are recorded for almost everyone by the Social Security system).[12] Once a worker's productivity status is determined, a subsidy sufficient to bring his value (to the employer) up to the standard that would permit his being paid the

Federal minimum wage (plus an amount adequate to compensate the employer for the expense of administering the subsidy) could be paid the employer. Further, in order to encourage employers to improve the productivity levels of these workers, the subsidy can be a declining one over time, say a five year period. Provision could also be made for an indefinite recycling of a permanently disadvantaged worker once his subsidy had declined to zero.

I have not provided all the details of a possible system of income supplementation through employer subsidies. However, enough information is there to indicate its feasibility. Now, what are the advantages of this approach? Two major ones, I would say. First, it could provide income supplementation at least sufficient to bring many people up to a level of income at least equal to that warranted by full time employment at the minimum wage level. Second, it would involve those who would be the indirect recipients of the income supplements in work activity. Hopefully, in at least some cases, there would be long-lasting beneficial effects associated with this involvement in the form of permanent enhancement of the productive abilities of the subsidized workers. To the extent that this happens, the employment subsidy approach is all the more advantageous. The important, almost critical thing, though, is the drawing of people into the normal patterns of economic life in the United States. This, at least, should have the effect of providing a greater sense of community between those who are subsidized and the remainder of the society. By contrast, income supplementation through the provision of pure transfer payment income amounts to nothing more than saying to certain people, "You don't have the abilities to compete successfully in our economy but, since we are nice pleasant souls, we will provide you with sufficient income to live at some minimally acceptable level." Patronizing, to say the least.

Now, what about the disadvantages? Surely, there must be some. The major one is that it does not provide for all the income supplementation that is required in our society. Obviously, this is not the appropriate way to deal with the problem of income maintenance for the aged. But, that is not where we face the basic dilemma of a conflict between the goal of income maintenance and the "work ethic." In fact, this is one area in which the present approach to providing income supplements seems to be producing beneficial results. Or, what about the need for income maintenance for female heads of households and minors? In the case of minor children, the employment subsidy approach is not useful. With female heads of household, I would expect it to be partially applicable. By increasing the earnings potential of low productivity women, it would serve to encourage their participation in the labor force. And, of course, for those who elect non-work activity, there is still the present system of income supplementation, imperfect as it is. This would leave us with a "mixed" system for providing income supplementation, but there is nothing necessarily wrong with that.

Some final remarks. In assessing the nature of the poverty problem in the United States, we have placed great emphasis on the importance of differentials in the distribution of genetic human capital as a source of inequality in the distribution of income. This implies something "natural" about the existence of relative poverty in this country. What it also strongly suggests is that if, collectively, we feel that the present level of income inequality is unacceptable, we will be forced to resort to income supplementation for the relatively disadvantaged in order to create an acceptable situation. This raises the fundamental question of whether the necessary income supplements can be provided without conflicting too strongly with the prevailing "work ethic" of the society. To our mind, it can be done with the mix of public policies we have suggested. Only the future will be able to judge whether we are correct in our judgment.

FOOTNOTES

[1] For a superb summary of Carlyle's views, see Gide, Charles, and Rist, Charles, *A History of Economic Doctrines*, Second English Edition, London: George C. Harrap & Co., 1948, pp. 541-542.

[2] The basic grimness of the "classical" economics derives in large part from the Malthusian population theory which suggests that population will expand in a fashion that will drive the wage rate toward the subsistence level.

[3] We would emphasize again the variety of recent research that supports this notion. For example, Jencks, *op. cit.*, de Wolfe and van Slijpe, *op. cit.*, and Taubman and Wales, *op. cit.*, provide substantial evidence to support this.

[4] The society's ambivalence, when faced with this prospect, is perhaps best illustrated by George McGovern's experience with his plan to provide everybody with a $1,000 a year transfer payment from the Federal Government.

[5] Attempting to attack this aspect of the problem of Negro-white income differentials by transfer payments to Negroes with income above a society wide income floor, would probably face severe constitutional challenges on the grounds that it discriminated according to race.

[6] There is some evidence that Negroes derive their labor market information largely through contacts with other Negroes. This could result in less information being available to them.

[7] This very thing is happening in the academic world. Pressure being exerted through the Federal Government to hire minorities is resulting in women having a preferred status in the academic labor market. Because their supply is somewhat limited, their price is being bid up

and they frequently have a wider range of choice in job opportunities than men of the same ability. In a real sense, many of them are earning "economic rent" as the result of their sex.

[8]Actually, in 1970, there were more families with a female head of household with poverty incomes than there were families living in poverty who had a Negro head of household (2,190,000 to 1,370,000). Source: *Current Population Reports, P-60 Series.*

[9]The characterization of the Social Security program as an "insurance" system was developed in the 1930's to convince legislators to enact the program. However, it has long since ceased to be an "insurance" system.

[10]To a certain extent, the "retirement" test that puts a limit on work activity by the aged receiving old age benefits under Social Security constitutes a "needs" test. In general, though, benefits are available as a matter of right.

[11]*Manpower Economics, op. cit.*, Chapter 10.

[12]For details of how this can be done, see *Manpower Economics, op. cit.*, Chapter 10.